STORIES
OF THE
HYMNS

RAWSON & TONIOLI

Tonioli.com

GlennRawsonStories.com

RAWSON & TONIOLI

©2021 Glenn J. Rawson, Jean Tonioli, and Jason Tonioli

ISBN 978-1-68524-250-3

Printed in the United States of America

10 9 8 7 6 5 4 3 2

TABLE OF CONTENTS

PROLOGUE

My Friends,

It is my personal belief that hymns are a form of worship and prayer, and are capable of expressing with power what mere words alone cannot. Moreover, sacred music has an almost incalculable power to soften hearts, invite the Spirit, teach truth, and bind us together in unity.

Behind each hymn is an author, a composer, and a story. The Almighty does not generally draw upon a dry well. It is out the depths of our own experiences that He calls us to minister to others, teach, write, and compose. We learned again and again while doing research for this book that the personal experiences of the authors and composers influenced the words and music they wrote. Each hymn and its message became so much more meaningful when we came to know the author and composer.

These stories are true and drawn from as many sources as we could acquire. There is always the challenge of mortal memory, inaccurate interpretations, and faulty documents, but we have done the best we could to cross-reference and check the facts.

It is our hope and prayer that this book will strengthen and affirm your faith, draw you closer to the Almighty, and cause you to sing with greater intent, more power, hope, and joy.

FORWARD

I can still remember sitting at the piano bench as a boy, with my mother telling me there would come a time when I would appreciate the ability to play the hymns from a hymn book and that others would be blessed by my musical talent. I wish I had the maturity then to value the efforts of my mom and piano teacher encouraging me to practice piano.

It is ironic that for the past 20 years, I have spent thousands of hours at a piano writing, arranging, and recording hundreds of piano solos and other music. More than half of the songs I have created have been hymn arrangements. My younger self on the piano bench would be surprised that my music has been played and listened to by millions of people.

I'm always looking for beautiful melodies and have found that some of the best music and melodies are found in old hymns. I've come to realize great music isn't tied to any specific religion or denomination, and that through the music you can help others to feel the Spirit.

This project started as an idea years ago with my music books, as I would attempt to share a small piece of the story behind how a hymn had been written. There was never enough space to share the full story though.

With the help of my friend, Glenn Rawson and my mother, Jean Tonioli, we have been able to research and write these stories. In some ways, I feel like we are seeing a proper end to what started as a "piano war" with my mom and me at the piano bench, with her prediction that one day the time spent practicing the hymns would pay off and bless the lives of others.

Hopefully her predictions are true, and these stories and the music that comes with them will help draw many people closer to the Savior.

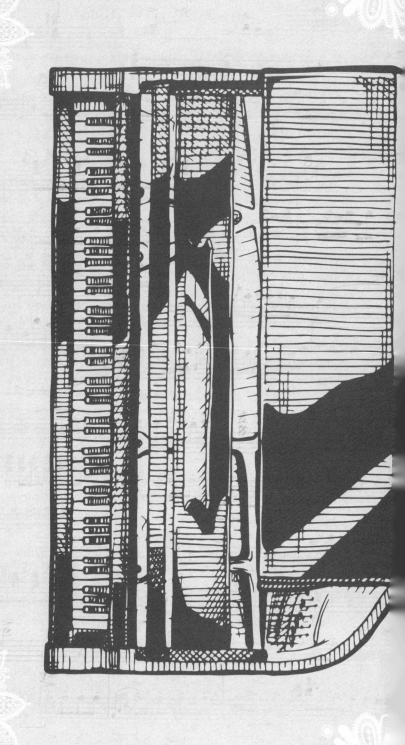

SABINE BARING-GOULD

CHAPTER ONE

A Children's Marching Song

It began in May 1864, when thirty-year-old Sabine Baring-Gould, newly ordained Anglican minister, set out for the small English community known as Horbury Bridge, where his calling was as curate or caretaker, and his charge was to open a new Church mission for children. He rented a cottage and established his school. Adults as well as children attended the school. Baring-Gould's purpose "was not just to educate and civilize people, but also to help them take on the Christian faith." He was very successful and within a short time a Mission Chapel was erected and opened in November 1865.

In that part of England at that time, the people celebrated Whitsun, which commemorated the Day of Pentecost in the Book of Acts. This holiday was marked with fairs, pageants, parades, and new clothes.

According to historical accounts, "In 1865, the vicar at St. Peter's church decided that the Horbury Bridge Mission scholars should join them. Baring-Gould was asked to conduct them to St. Peter's and the route from Horbury Bridge was then, as it is now, up Quarry Hill and beyond for over a mile. Fearful the little ones would straggle all over the place when climbing Quarry Hill, Baring-Gould decided singing a hymn would help make the children's long journey that much easier."

According to Baring-Gould's own account:

> "I had resolved that the [Bridge] children should come up to the parish church on Whitsun Tuesday. Mr. Fred Knowles came to me at the vicarage and asked what they should sing on the day of the long walk. We discussed one thing and then another, then I said, 'I'll write a processional.' Mr. Knowles replied, 'You must be sharp about it, as this is Saturday and there will shortly be no printing done.' So, I sat down and wrote the hymn. It was printed, practiced on the Sunday afternoon, and it was sung to the tune of Haydn on the Tuesday."

According to various accounts, Baring-Gould sat up all night struggling with what to write for the forthcoming march and finally, in a flash of inspiration, he either composed or completed some lines, borrowed a tune, and went to face his students. It was printed and distributed to his young charges. They quickly learned it, and on the appointed day, marched up the hill singing the processional song that Reverend Sabine Baring-Gould never intended to publish. It was meant for that day and only to inspire and impress upon his students that they were soldiers for Christ after the manner spoken of by the Apostle Paul when he said to Timothy, "Thou therefore endure hardness, as a good soldier of Jesus Christ."

The students sang:

> *Onward, Christian soldiers,*
> *Marching as to war,*
> *With the cross of Jesus*
> *Going on before!*
> *Christ, the royal Master,*

Leads against the foe;
Forward into battle,
See his banner go!

Years later, Sabine Baring-Gould would say of that hymn:

> "It was written in great haste, and I am afraid some of
> the rhymes are faulty. Certainly nothing has surprised
> me more than its popularity. I don't remember how it
> got printed first, but I know that very soon it found
> its way into several collections. I have written a few
> other hymns since then, but only two or three have
> become at all well known."

In 1871, the great composer, Arthur Sullivan, set the words to a
new tune widely sung by Christians today. That song, intended
to inspire faith and courage in children, has become one of the
most beloved hymns of all time. Who can measure how many
hearts have been inspired with courage by the simple gift of a
children's processional hymn?

PART II

One such memorable moment in the history of this great
hymn occurred in August 1941, when United States President
Franklin Delano Roosevelt sailed to a secret location in the
north Atlantic to meet with British Prime Minister Winston
Churchill. Roosevelt eluded reporters under cover of darkness
and went to rendezvous with Churchill aboard the British
battleship *Prince of Wales*.

This was a critical meeting. England was fighting with its back
against the wall, determined to stand against Nazi Germany
at all costs. The United States had not yet entered the war,

but their help was sorely needed. The two men talked for four days. Then on Sunday, Roosevelt was transported to the *Prince of Wales* for a morning church service. All the fighting men aboard, together with two of the most powerful leaders on earth, met on the quarterdeck for a worship service for which Prime Minister Churchill chose the hymns—his favorites. The effect of that inspiring service, as Roosevelt described it, "cemented us." Among the hymns sung that morning was "Onward Christian Soldiers." Churchill would later describe that morning as "A great hour to live." In a subsequent radio broadcast, Churchill spoke of this meeting and of that hymn.

> "We sang "Onward, Christian Soldiers" indeed, and I felt that this was no vain presumption, but that we had the right to feel that we were serving a cause for the sake of which a trumpet has sounded from on high. When I looked upon that densely packed congregation of fighting men of the same language, of the same faith, of the same fundamental laws, of the same ideals ... it swept across me that here was the only hope, but also the sure hope, of saving the world from measureless degradation."

Sources:

https://en.wikipedia.org/wiki/Whitsun

https://www.ossett.net/beyond/Sabine_Baring_Gould.html

2 Timothy 2:3 KJV

https://www.challies.com/articles/hymn-stories-onward-christian-soldiers/

https://reasonabletheology.org/hymn-story-onward-christian-soldiers/

https://en.wikipedia.org/wiki/Onward,_Christian_Soldiers

JOHN NEWTON

CHAPTER TWO

JOHN NEWTON

John Newton was born July 24, 1725, in London, England. His father was a sea captain and his mother a pious dissenter from the Church of England. Life may have taken a completely different course for John had his mother lived long enough for her teachings to take root, but she died when he was only six. His father, gone at sea, left his care to an indifferent step-mother. John ran wild.

Then, at age 11, John went to sea with his father, drinking in the ways of the sailor. After six voyages, John's father retired. By the age of 17, John was characterized as headstrong and disobedient, and despite his father's efforts to establish him as a prosperous merchantman, John rebelled and soon found himself kidnapped, or pressed into service, in the Royal Navy.

Not to be cowed, John deserted, but was soon captured, flogged, and enslaved on the ship. As fate would have it, John was traded to a slave ship, and soon found himself bound for Africa and a cargo of slaves. Due to his own insolence, his situation gravely worsened over time and John became a servant of the slaves, starved and abused. The slaves pitied him, smuggling food into him and letters out to his father.

Finally, his father found him and he was freed. It would be assumed that life's experiences and the lingering tug of his childhood faith would have softened John's heart, but it did not. He became once more shockingly profane and debauched. Then on the night of March 21, 1748, the ship he

was on sailed into a violent storm. Men were washed overboard. The ship pitched and rolled and seemed as though it would capsize. John lashed himself to the pumps, commenting to the captain, "If this will not do, then Lord have mercy upon us."

The flippant remark latched onto John's soul and would not let go. He reflected on it all night, finally uttering his first weak prayer. He would later declare this was "the hour he first believed." The ship survived the storm.

John's faith ebbed and flowed, finally rooting deep and setting him on a course of humility and goodness that would last out his days. It took time, but he gave up the sea and the slave trade, turning instead to the study of languages and theology. He wanted to be a clergyman, but was turned down because he had no university degree. At last though, he was sponsored and ordained a minister.

John Newton became one of the most powerful and persuasive clergymen of his time. Why? It was because he was passionate and personal when he spoke of sin and Christ's redemptive power. He knew his own weakness and when he spoke of the Lord's mercy and grace, it was from the depth of a grateful heart.

Not content in the boundaries of his own parish, he traveled and taught all who would listen. Sunday meetings were not enough to meet the need and he began to hold weekly prayer meetings to bolster the faith of the poor around him. Ironically, it was a young man taught and influenced by Newton who would become himself a clergyman, a member of Parliament, and influence Great Britain to outlaw the slave trade—William Wilberforce.

However, it is not for the converts Newton made that he is most remembered. This profane wretch, who once wondered at sea in a deadly storm if he had sinned too much—if heaven

still had a place for him, is most remembered today for a hymn that he wrote for a prayer meeting. It was sung for the first time January 1, 1773. That hymn was "Amazing Grace"—the spiritual autobiography of John Newton, the sailor.

> *Amazing Grace, how sweet the sound*
> *That saved a wretch like me.*
> *I once was lost, but now am found*
> *Was blind but now I see.*
>
> *Was Grace that taught my heart to fear*
> *And Grace, my fears relieved;*
> *How precious did that Grace appear*
> *The hour I first believed!*
>
> *Through many dangers, toils and snares*
> *We have already come:*
> *Tis grace that brought us safe thus far*
> *And grace will lead us home.*

Sources:

https://hymnary.org/text/amazing_grace_how_sweet_the_sound

https://www.biography.com/news/amazing-grace-story-john-newton

ROBERT ROBINSON

CHAPTER THREE

COME THOU FOUNT OF EVERY BLESSING

Robert Robinson was born in Norfolk, England in September 1735. When he was just eight years old, his father passed away. Though of tender years, Robert was apprenticed to a barber and labored to support himself and his mother. His grandfather, a man of means, disinherited him because of his mother's low marriage. Robert's opportunities for education were limited, but he sought to learn. He was described as "more given to reading than to his profession."

Robert's mother was said to be a goodly woman and desired that her son become a clergyman. Notwithstanding that lofty ambition, Robert fell into a crowd that was bent on drunken and debauched living. Then in 1752, a series of events brought him up short:

> "Out on a frolic one Sunday with like-minded companions, he joined with them in sportively rendering a fortune-telling old woman drunk and incapable, that they might hear and laugh at her predictions concerning them. The poor creature told Robinson that he would live to see his children and grandchildren. This set him a-thinking, and he resolved more than ever to 'give himself to reading.'"

Around this same time he went to hear the famed Methodist preacher, George Whitefield.

Whitefield's text was the Lord's words, "O generation of vipers. Who hath warned you to flee from the wrath to come? "(Matthew 3:7). The powerful sermon struck a chord with the young man and haunted him. "For three years he walked in darkness and fear, but in his 20th year found peace by believing."

Robert Robinson had made his peace with God. He continued studying, listening, and learning with an assiduous intent. He first preached as a Methodist, and then in 1759 accepted baptism and as time progressed became a powerful and popular Baptist minister and scholar.

It is difficult, perhaps impossible, for a writer to compose and not insert himself—his thoughts, feelings, and desires—into the text. It is for that reason the hymn composed by Robinson when he was only 22 years old is thought to be autobiographical. Consider these words from a young man who only recently found the Savior.

> *Come thou fount of every blessing*
> *Tune my heart to sing thy grace*
> *Streams of mercy, never ceasing*
> *Call for songs of loudest praise.*
> *Teach me some melodious sonnet*
> *Sung by flaming tongues above.*
> *I'll praise the mount, I'm fixed upon it*
> *Mount of thy redeeming love.*

Late in his life, Robinson changed religious persuasions again, aligning himself with a third faith. Could it be that he understood his own impulsive instability, giving added meaning to the most powerful and enduring words he ever wrote?

Prone to wander, Lord, I feel it.
Prone to leave the God I love.
Here's my heart, O take and seal it,
Seal it for thy courts above.

Sources:

https://hymnary.org/person/Robinson_R?tab=hymnals

https://www.staugustine.com/article/20150917lifesty le/309179974

HORATIO SPAFFORD

CHAPTER FOUR

HORATIO SPAFFORD

Horatio Spafford came to Chicago in 1856 to practice law. He was a devoutly religious man and soon formed associations with other evangelical Christians. In those early days in Chicago, Spafford put his Christianity into practice, teaching Sunday School classes, visiting the sick and imprisoned, and ministering where he could.

In 1857, he first met Anna Larsson, a recent immigrant from Norway. He was taken with her beauty and confidence. However, she was only 15 years old. Spafford paid for Anna to attend an elite women's school. After graduation three years later, they were married.

During the Civil War, Horatio and Anna volunteered and served where they could. Horatio continued as a lawyer, senior partner in their firm, and as a professor of law. In 1870, their four-year-old son, Horatio Jr., died of scarlet fever. Then, a year later in October 1871, the great Chicago fire reduced Chicago to ashes, taking with it most of Horatio's considerable real estate investments. Notwithstanding their loss, the Spaffords worked to assist others stricken by the fire.

In 1873, the family decided to take a holiday to England. Horatio was detained because of business in the city and sent his wife and four remaining children ahead. This included Anna and her eleven-year-old daughter, also named Anna, nine-year-old Margaret, five-year-old Elizabeth, and two-year-old Tanetta.

On November 22, 1873, their ship, the *Ville Du Havre*, was rammed midships by another vessel, the *Lochearn*, and sank in 12 minutes. It was one of the worst maritime disasters in the 19th century, as 226 people lost their lives. Among them were the four daughters of Horatio and Anna Spafford. At the collision, Anna gathered her children close, looked for escape, and attempted to comfort and assist other passengers. However, as the ship tipped onto its bow and started under, the babe Tanetta was torn from her arms and swept away, as were the other girls. In the end, the four girls either drowned or succumbed to the icy waters of the North Atlantic. Anna was found floating semi-conscious on a piece of planking. After her rescue, she was overheard to say, "God gave me four daughters. Now they have been taken from me. Someday I will understand why." She would later testify that in anguish and grief, she heard a still small voice speaking to her, "You were saved for a purpose."

When she arrived in Cardiff, South Wales, she sent a telegram to her husband that read simply, "Saved alone. What shall I do?"

Horatio immediately boarded a ship and set out to join Anna. As they sailed, it is reported that one day, the captain called Spafford to the bridge, pointed to his navigation charts, and informed him they were passing over the very spot where the *Ville du Havre* went down. Spafford returned to his cabin and, with emotions we can only imagine, wrote these words:

> *When peace, like a river, attendeth my way,*
> *When sorrows like sea billows roll;*
> *Whatever my lot, Thou hast taught me to say,*
> *It is well, it is well with my soul.*

Refrain:

It is well with my soul,
It is well, it is well with my soul.

Though Satan should buffet, though trials should come,
Let this blest assurance control,
That Christ hath regarded my helpless estate,
And hath shed His own blood for my soul.

My sin—oh, the bliss of this glorious thought!—
My sin, not in part but the whole,
Is nailed to the cross, and I bear it no more,
Praise the Lord, praise the Lord, O my soul!

For me, be it Christ, be it Christ hence to live:
If Jordan above me shall roll,
No pang shall be mine, for in death as in life
Thou wilt whisper Thy peace to my soul.

But, Lord, 'tis for Thee, for Thy coming we wait,
The sky, not the grave, is our goal;
Oh, trump of the angel! Oh, voice of the Lord!
Blessed hope, blessed rest of my soul!

And Lord, haste the day when the faith shall be sight,
The clouds be rolled back as a scroll;
The trump shall resound, and the Lord shall descend,
Even so, it is well with my soul.

A few days later, his faith shone through again as he wrote in a letter, "On Thursday last, we passed over the spot where she went down, in mid-ocean, the waters three miles deep. But I do not think of our dear ones there. They are safe.... dear lambs."

The Spaffords returned to Chicago where three more children were born to them, but, like Job, was it the end of their loss and sorrow? No! Their only surviving son died at the age of four. It is said that people of their congregation began to talk ill saying, "What had the Spaffords done to so offend God and bring upon themselves so much misfortune?"

Horatio and Anna Spafford left Chicago, and their church, emigrating to Jerusalem where they established the famous American Colony. There Horatio and Anna lived out their days practicing the full measure of Christianity as they knew it. All were loved and served, and all were welcomed and ministered to. They gave all they had and in a land of enemies and allies, they took no sides. Horatio and Anna Spafford are both buried in Jerusalem, awaiting that day they so longed for when the Lord would return and call them up. Indeed, it is well with their souls.

Sources:

https://www.bethelripon.com/life-stories/horatio-gates-spafford

https://www.loc.gov/exhibits/americancolony/amcolony-family.html

https://en.wikipedia.org/wiki/It_Is_Well_with_My_Soul

https://www.loc.gov/exhibits/americancolony/amcolony-family.html

Ludwig Van Beethoven

CHAPTER FIVE

JOY

Most people recognize the name Beethoven, and there are few that would not recognize his Ninth Symphony, which he wrote when he could no longer hear. What people may not know is how Beethoven, the deaf composer, was inspired to use a poem that never translated well into English. That composition, as part of his symphony, would later become one of our most well recognized hymns.

Ludwig van Beethoven (1770-1827), had a lot of creative energy, but was wrestling with a huge handicap. The musician, who was one of the greatest composers of all time, had lost his ability to hear. How could a musician who couldn't test out the harmonies he wrote be able to produce any music? Despite his inability to hear, Beethoven persevered with writing a colossal work—his Symphony No. 9. In addition to being longer and more complex than anything he'd written so far, he planned to include a chorus and vocal soloists in the final movement. He would be the first major composer to do this in a symphony. Recalling a poem called "An die Freude," which was written in 1785 by Friedrich Schiller, he used the text as the words for the singers. He titled the song "Ode to Joy."

The Ninth Symphony was first performed on May 7, 1824, at Vienna's Karntnertorm Theater. Beethoven was totally deaf, but stood next to the conductor to indicate the proper tempo for each part of the work. The performance was a resounding

success, combining the orchestra and singers. It was received with a great deal of enthusiasm and emotion, not only by the audience, but more unusually by the orchestra. Thunderous applause came from the listeners—but Beethoven stood with his back to the audience, unaware of the resounding acceptance of the music written by a deaf composer. One of the soloists turned him around to face the people, and an expression of sympathy, tears, and admiration followed, with applause which seemed to never end. Symphony No. 9 and the magnificent performance of "Ode to Joy" produced a celebration of "joy" that no one in the concert hall would ever forget.

The melody to the song "Ode to Joy" became well known and loved throughout the world. Written in German, the lyrics of the much-admired poem were later translated into English. As often happens when translating lyrics into another language, the text did not flow well and was not as impactful with English speaking audiences.

An American, Henry van Dyke (1852-1933), admired Beethoven's celebrated melody. He was born at Germantown, Pennsylvania in 1852. During his lifetime, Van Dyke was a well-known Presbyterian preacher, a Navy Chaplain during World War I, and an American ambassador to Holland and Luxembourg. He worked for 23 years as a professor of English literature at Princeton and was a prolific writer.

While serving as a guest preacher in 1907 at Williams College, Van Dyke wrote the text to a new song. His son, Tertius, gave this explanation of how the text came about:

> "Just before a service in the Williams College Chapel, President Garfield told me how the hymn came to be written. My father was staying in Garfield's home. One morning when he came down to breakfast, he put the manuscript of the hymn on the table, saying:

'Here is a hymn for you. Your mountains (the Berkshires) were my inspiration. It must be sung to the music of Beethoven's *'Hymn to Joy.'*"

Henry van Dyke was a man who was well acquainted with God and his relationship with the Lord was a great source of joy to him. Van Dyke later stated his purpose in writing this hymn:

"These verses are simple expressions of common Christian feelings and desires in this present time, hymns of today that may be sung together by people who know the thought of the age, and are not afraid that any truth of science will destroy their religion or that any revolution on earth will overthrow the kingdom of heaven."

Acknowledging the efforts of the German poet, Schiller, who wrote the words which Beethoven used in his Symphony No. 9, Van Dyke presented his English text which described the joy he experienced from praising God. Joining with Beethoven's melody for "Ode to Joy", he created a beautiful hymn. First published in 1911, this beloved hymn has been published in 284 hymnals and recorded by artists around the world. Two of the four verses are:

Joyful, joyful, we adore Thee
God of glory, Lord of love.
Hearts unfold like flowers before Thee
Opening to the sun above.
Melt the clouds of sin and sadness
Drive the dark of doubt away.
Giver of immortal gladness
Fill us with the light of day.
Mortals join the mighty chorus

Which the morning stars began.
Father-love is reigning o'er us
Brother-love binds man to man.
Ever singing, march we onward
Victors in the midst of strife.
Joyful music lifts us sunward
In the triumph song of life.

It has been said that "Music is God's gift to man, the only art of Heaven given to earth, the only art of earth we take to Heaven." Surely the angels in heaven will continue to praise the Lord by singing "Ode to Joy."

Sources:

https://www.mbarikiwamedia.com/2020/06/10/story-behind-the-hymn-joyful-joyful-we-adore-thee/

https://www.classicfm.com/composers/beethoven/music/symphony-no-9-d-minor/

https://www.brainyquote.com/authors/walter-savage-landor-quotes

https://en.wikipedia.org/wiki/The_Hymn_of_Joy

https://hymnary.org/text/joyful_joyful_we_adore_thee

FANNY HUMPHRIES

CHAPTER SIX

FANNY HUMPHRIES

Fanny Humphries was a talented, yet humble young woman who cultivated from a young age a desire to love and serve others in the Lord's name. Fanny especially loved children and spent much of her life ministering to their needs. In 1846, she helped establish a school for deaf and dumb children. She helped set up institutions to assist nurses and even labored to minister to that shamed class that society so often shunned—fallen women. She ministered to the care of the poor and needy, especially the children, all her life. Her kindness and indefatigable service live on to the present day. Long after she was gone, those who knew her remembered her walking to the farthest reaches carrying food and bringing love, and returning home in the most inclement weather, soaked through. Her motives in all of this were not the honor and praise of the world. Duncan Campbell said of her:

> "[She] was deaf to applause, but when someone wrote to tell of a great change in heart and life that had come to a worldly man through hearing this hymn sung, she sprang from her chair exclaiming, 'Thank God! I do like to hear that.' Those, however, who knew her best felt that, beautiful as her hymns are, her life was more beautiful still."

From the time she was just a child, Fanny loved to write. Encouraged by her father and later her husband, she would compose more than 400 hymns in her lifetime. Her first

book of hymns was for children. It was titled *"Hymns for Little Children."*

The proceeds of that first book were used to help the needy. Fanny's desire was to bring souls to Christ—to teach in so simple and plain a way that children could understand. She knew that to teach a child you must first capture their imagination with the picturesque and then explain in the simplest of terms. One of her most enduring and beloved hymns was reportedly written by the bedside of a sick child. It was an inspired effort to explain why the Savior had to die—why it was necessary that the pure Son of Almighty God had to be crucified to save us all.

It is believed that Fanny looked beyond the city walls of Derry, Ireland and saw in the Creggan Hills, "a green hill far away." With that imagery, she taught in powerful plainness, the most eternally fundamental doctrine of them all—the atonement of the Lord Jesus Christ. It has been called "the most perfect hymn in the English language." She wrote:

> *There is a green hill far away,*
> *Without a city wall,*
> *Where the dear Lord was crucified,*
> *Who died to save us all.*

Fanny Humpheries grew up to be Cecil Frances Alexander, the Bishop's wife and a faithful servant of the Lord she loved. She lived these very words she wrote.

> *Oh, dearly, dearly has He loved!*
> *And we must love Him too,*

And trust in His redeeming blood,
And try His works to do.

She died in 1895, very much beloved by all those upon whom she did the Lord's works. She was buried in Derry Cemetery, on the very "green hill far away" that she wrote of, awaiting the day of a glorious resurrection. The other hymn for which we so often remember her—"He is Risen!"—the spiritual anthem of Easter.

Sources:

https://www.stempublishing.com/hymns/biographies/alexander.html

https://www.poemhunter.com/cecil-frances-alexander/biography/

https://www.hymnologyarchive.com/cecil-frances-alexander

https://willchapumc.org/images/Worship/allthingsbrightandbeautiful.pdf

https://www.gantshillurc.co.uk/ministers-blog/the-hymns-of-cecil-frances-alexander

https://www.methodist.org.uk/our-faith/worship/singing-the-faith-plus/hymns/there-is-a-green-hill-far-away-stf-284/

https://oystermouthparish.com/hymn-of-the-month-there-is-a-green-hill

ROBERT LOWRY

CHAPTER SEVEN

THE RELUCTANT HYMN WRITER

The people of New York City were having a very difficult time during the summer of 1864. The Civil War was raging, fracturing the nation and leaving families anxiously waiting for any news from the battlefront. The heat and humidity were relentless. Just when people thought they had reached the height of misery, an epidemic swept through the city, with fever and death taking a toll.

Thirty-eight-year-old Rev. Robert Lowry was the pastor of the Hanson Place Baptist Church in Brooklyn. One evening, after an exhausting day of visiting some of the sick and dying members of his church community, he thought of the scripture in Revelations 22:1 which described "…a pure river of water of life, clear as crystal, proceeding out of the throne of God and the Lamb." He wondered why some hymn writers did not focus their songs on the truth that friends and loved ones could be reunited one day at this beautiful river. The words of the hymn, "Shall We Gather at the River?" came to him and he quickly wrote them down. Then, he sat down at his parlor organ and composed the tune:

> *Shall we gather at the river,*
> *Where bright angel-feet have trod,*
> *With its crystal tide forever*
> *Flowing by the throne of God?*

Chorus:

Yes, we'll gather at the river,
The beautiful, the beautiful river;
Gather with the saints at the river
That flows by the throne of God.

A reporter once asked Robert Lowry what his method was for writing hymns. His reply was:

> "I have no method. Sometimes the music comes and the words follow, fitted insensibly to the melody. I watch my moods, and when anything good strikes me, whether words or music, and no matter where I am, at home or on the street, I jot it down. Often the margin of a newspaper or the back of an envelope serves as a notebook. My brain is a sort of spinning machine, I think, for there is music running through it all the time. I do not pick out my music on the keys of an instrument. The tunes of nearly all the hymns I have written have been completed on paper before I tried them on the organ. Frequently the words of the hymn and the music have been written at the same time."

Rev. Lowry is credited with writing more than 500 hymn tunes, often composing the text and music. However, he was reluctant to accept the title of hymn writer. He claimed that he would rather preach a gospel sermon to an appreciative congregation than write a hymn and that writing hymns was a mere hobby. He even once said that he felt a sense of loss that he came to be more well known for his hymns instead of his preaching.

Robert Lowry told the following story about "Shall We Gather at the River?"

> "It is brass-band music, has a march movement, and for that reason has become popular, though, for myself, I do not think much of it. Yet on several occasions I have been deeply moved by the singing of this very hymn. Going from Harrisburg to Lewisburg once, I got into a car filled with half-drunken lumbermen. Suddenly, one of them struck up, 'Shall We Gather at the River?' And they sang it over and over again, repeating the chorus in a wild, boisterous way. I did not think so much of the music then, as I listened to those singers; but I did think that perhaps the spirit of the hymn, the words so flippantly uttered, might somehow survive and be carried forward into the lives of those careless men, and ultimately lift them upward to the realization of the hope expressed in the hymn."

In 1880, he attended a meeting in England which celebrated the 100th anniversary of the establishment of Sunday Schools by Robert Raikes:

> "I was in London, and had gone to a meeting in the Old Bailey to see some of the most famous Sunday-school workers of the world. They were present from Europe, Asia, and America. I sat in a rear seat alone. After there had been a number of addresses delivered in various languages, I was preparing to leave, when the chairman of the meeting announced that the author of 'Shall We Gather at the River?' was present, and I was requested by name to come forward. Men applauded and women waved their handkerchiefs as I went to the platform. It was a tribute to the hymn;

but I felt, after it was over, that I had perhaps done some little good in the world."

Rev. Robert Lowry died at his home in Plainfield, N.J. in 1899. However, the reluctant hymn writer's legacy today is not in the sermons he preached from the pulpit, but the hymns where he so ably preached the gospel through song. He is most famously known today for that hymn he did not think much of—"Shall We Gather at the River?"—It has been printed in 695 hymnals, translated into many languages, and sung throughout the Christian world.

Sources:

https://anahernandez.org/shall-we-gather-at-the-river-2/

Hall, J. H. (1914). Biography of Gospel Song and Hymn Writers. New York: Fleming H. Revell, (pp. 132–133).

https://www.hymnologyarchive.com/shall-we-gather

http://songscoops.blogspot.com/2017/01/shall-we-gather-at-river-robert-lowry.html

https://www.wholesomewords.org/biography/blowry.html

Julia Ward Howe

CHAPTER EIGHT

THAT STIRRING TUNE

The date was November 1861. The Civil War was just beginning. Samuel Gridley Howe and his wife, Julia, both fervent abolitionists, traveled to Washington, D.C. to meet with President Abraham Lincoln. Howe was appointed by Lincoln as part of a Military Sanitation Committee. As part of their visit, the Howes took occasion to review the troops stationed near Washington, D. C. They heard the troops singing some of the popular fight songs of the day. One of those was a repurposed Methodist camp song titled by the soldiers, "John Brown's Body." The song was catchy and wildly popular among the soldiers, even if the lyrics were less than uplifting. One of which read, "Let's hang Jeff Davis from a sour apple tree."

After the review, the party returned to the city surrounded by soldiers and all began singing the songs of the war. They had completed a rendition of "John Brown's Body" when the Reverend James Freeman Clarke commented to Mrs. Howe,

"Mrs. Howe, why do you not write some good words for that stirring tune?"

"I have often wished to do so!" she replied.

Julie Ward Howe was forty-two years old, a wife and a mother of six. She was also an educated and accomplished writer who yearned to do something that aided a war effort she deeply believed in. The party returned to the city and

to their lodgings in the Willard Hotel. It was on that night of November 19, 1861, that Julia Ward Howe later described what happened:

"I went to bed that night as usual, and slept, according to my wont, quite soundly. I awoke in the gray of the morning twilight, and as I lay waiting for the dawn, the long lines of the desired poem began to twine themselves in my mind. Having thought out all the stanzas, I said to myself, 'I must get up and write these verses down, lest I fall asleep again and forget them.' So, with a sudden effort, I sprang out of bed, and found in the dimness an old stump of a pencil which I remembered to have used the day before. I scrawled the verses almost without looking at the paper."

It is one of the happy ironies of history that out of a crass war song came a hymn which would become the unofficial national anthem of the United States of America—"The Battle Hymn of the Republic."

Mine eyes have seen the glory
Of the coming of the Lord,
He is trampling out the vintage
Where the grapes of wrath are stored,
He hath loosed the fateful lightning
Of His terrible swift sword,
His truth is marching on.
Glory, Glory Hallelujah!
Glory, Glory Hallelujah!
Glory, Glory Hallelujah!
His truth is marching on.

And by the way, the words and spirit of that rousing hymn were not hollow hyperbole for their author. Julia Ward Howe would fight all her days for those causes that lifted society and made it better. She died at the age of 91 and is buried in Cambridge Massachusetts. At her funeral, 4,000 people sang "The Battle Hymn of the Republic" in tribute to her life.

Sources:

https://en.wikipedia.org/wiki/Julia_Ward_Howe

https://www.theatlantic.com/entertainment/archive/2010/11/the-battle-hymn-of-the-republic-americas-song-of-itself/66070/

https://www.npr.org/2018/07/04/625351953/one-song-glory
http://digital.library.upenn.edu/women/richards/howe/howe-I.html

JOSEPH SCRIVEN

CHAPTER NINE

JOSEPH SCRIVEN: THE GOOD MAN

The story is told of a large man with a pleasant countenance walking along the streets of Lake Rice, Canada carrying a sawhorse and a bucksaw. "That looks like a sober man. I think I'll hire him to cut wood for me," said one of the town's more prosperous residents. "That's Joseph Scriven," said another man. "He wouldn't cut wood for you because you can afford to hire him. He only cuts wood for those who don't have enough money to pay." Indeed, and so it was true.

Joseph Medlicott Scriven was known in the community as "the good man." "For years he tended the cow of a Port Hope widow and carried the milk to her customers; he sawed wood for those who could not pay; he sold his watch, brought from Ireland, to replace someone's lost cow; and more than he could well spare he gave to the needy." He went about doing good in emulation of the Master he loved. Who was this man and how did he come to be here?

Joseph was born September 10, 1819 near Dublin, Ireland. His father was a military man and when Joseph came of age, he enrolled in a military college near London, but was soon forced to withdraw for reasons of health. He entered Trinity College Dublin where he received a B.A. degree in 1842. While there, Joseph became engaged to the love of his life, but on the night before they were to be wed, she was thrown from her horse while crossing the River Bann and knocked unconscious. She drowned before Joseph could save her.

Whether it was his grief or his newfound faith among the Plymouth Brethren, Joseph became a preacher and a wanderer. He emigrated to Canada, where he tutored children, preached, and ministered to the poor.

By 1857, he was living near Port Hope, Ontario, Canada and tutoring in the household of Robert Lamport Pengelly. It was while there that he met and fell in love with Pengelly's niece, Eliza Catherine Roach. They were engaged to be married, when Eliza suddenly passed away of pneumonia.

The sorrowful Joseph Scriven would not marry and lived out his days in Canada, pouring out his life, love, and service to all who needed him. He died in 1886 near Bewdley, Ontario, Canada.

Monuments and memorials have been erected both in Ontario and Dublin to honor and remember Joseph Medlicott Scriven, but it is not for his life of service that he is so justly remembered, but for a poem he wrote in 1855 that he never intended to publish. While living in Bewdley, he learned that his mother was ill in Ireland and in an effort to administer to the dear one that he could not go to, he wrote a letter containing the following verses which he titled "Pray Without Ceasing."

What a friend we have in Jesus, all our sins and griefs to bear!

What a privilege to carry everything to God in prayer!

O what peace we often forfeit, O what needless pain we bear,

All because we do not carry everything to God in prayer.

Have we trials and temptations? Is there trouble anywhere?

We should never be discouraged; take it to the Lord in prayer.

Can we find a friend so faithful who will all our sorrows share?

Jesus knows our every weakness; take it to the Lord in prayer.

Are we weak and heavy laden, cumbered with a load of care?

Precious Savior, still our refuge, take it to the Lord in prayer.

Do your friends despise, forsake you? Take it to the Lord in prayer!

In His arms He'll take and shield you; you will find a solace there.

Blessed Savior, Thou hast promised Thou wilt all our burdens bear

May we ever, Lord, be bringing all to Thee in earnest prayer.

Soon in glory bright unclouded there will be no need for prayer.

Rapture, praise and endless worship will be our sweet portion there.

Joseph never intended that his humble poem be published, but it was later found and set to music and became one of the most popular Christian hymns of all time—"What A Friend We Have in Jesus."

Perhaps it is that only those who have known suffering and service as the Lord Jesus gave it, can really know Jesus as Lord, Savior, Master—and friend.

Sources:

https://reasonabletheology.org/hymn-story-friend-jesus/

http://www.biographi.ca/en/bio/scriven_joseph_medlicott_11E.html

https://kidtunz.com/history-behind-the-hymn-what-a-friend-we-have-in-jesus/

http://www.biographi.ca/en/bio/scriven_joseph_medlicott_11E.html

https://en.wikipedia.org/wiki/Joseph_M._Scriven

MARTIN LUTHER

CHAPTER TEN

MARTIN LUTHER

Martin Luther was born in 1483 in Saxony, Germany, the son of prosperous parents. His father wanted him to pursue a career in law, but six weeks after enrolling in that course he withdrew and entered the monastery to become a monk. Notwithstanding his father's anger, Luther stayed his course. By May 1507, he was ordained to the priesthood. He returned to university studies in theology and obtained a doctorate and professorship in theology and biblical studies.

In 1517, Luther protested in writing the church practice of selling indulgences. While his Ninety-five Theses angered church leadership, it inspired the peasants and common folk across Germany. He was called to account for his actions and beliefs. When he refused to recant, an order was given for his arrest and Luther went into hiding. In 1519, Luther was excommunicated and shortly after branded a heretic. Such a designation would have made his life forfeit, but a number of factors combined to spare his life.

He was called again to account for his teachings and writings at a meeting of the Diet (assembly) of the Holy Roman Empire held at Worms, Germany in April 1521. He was asked to renounce his writings and recant his teachings. He refused, saying, "Here I stand. I can do no other. God help me. Amen."

By now, Luther was the enemy of the church as well as the Holy Roman Empire. Pope and Emperor wanted him dead, but his favor among the masses swelled. His ideas were caught up and carried—unfortunately, to violence and rioting. Luther stood and condemned the violent actions of the mobs. By 1530, Luther stood firmly in opposition against the church, against the Empire, against mob violence, and even other reformers who discredited his doctrine. He was an outlaw on the run and a heretic, but a man driven by conviction to his principles. He became the catalyst for the Protestant Reformation. About 1527, Luther who was a prolific writer and gifted hymnist, wrote the words and music to the following hymn translated into English:

A mighty fortress is our God,
A tower of strength ne'er failing.
A helper mighty is our God,
O'er ills of life prevailing.
He overcometh all.
He saveth from the Fall.
His might and pow'r are great.
He all things did create.
And he shall reign for evermore.

That hymn became known as the "Battle Hymn of the Reformation." It was an anthem of inspiration for exiles, martyrs, warriors, and nations. Translated and published in over 600 hymnals, it is one of the most popular Christian hymns of all time. One writer said of the hymn:

"It has had a part in countless celebrations commemorating the men and events of the

Reformation; and its first line is engraved on the base of Luther's monument at Wittenberg…An imperishable hymn! Not polished and artistically wrought, but rugged and strong like Luther himself, whose very words seem like deeds" (Albert Bailey, The Gospel in Hymns, 316).

Sources:

https://hymnary.org/text/a_mighty_fortress_is_our_god_a_bulwark

https://www.britannica.com/biography/Martin-Luther

Bailey, E. (1950). The Gospel in Hymns. Charles Scribner's Sons, New York.

BENJAMIN MANSELL RAMSEY

CHAPTER ELEVEN

TEACH ME THY WAY

The words and music of a sacred hymn can be a way to express what the heart feels during challenging times of life, and especially in the loss of a loved one. One English composer was longing for the Lord's comfort during such a time.

Benjamin Mansell Ramsey (1849-1923) was born in Richmond, Surrey, England. He married Edith Fairbrother and together they had six children – Bernard, Percy, Lilian, Harold, Wilfred, and Lawrence. As an adult, he became a well-known music teacher at Bournemouth Grammar School. He was a composer of part-songs, piano pieces, and mostly secular music. His works for children included Robinson Crusoe, A Cantata or Operetta for Boys in 1896 and Clouds and Sunshine: A Fairy Play. He helped establish an amateur orchestra which later became the Bournemouth Symphony Orchestra. He was secretary of the Bournemouth Musical Association.

Benjamin Ramsey retired from public life in 1916 and in 1919, four years before his death, wrote the words and music for the hymn "Teach Me Thy Way, O Lord." He called the hymn tune Camacha. The hymn is based on Psalm 27:11 which reads, "Teach me thy way, O Lord, and lead me in a plain path…". The first verse of the song is as follows:

Teach me Thy way, O Lord, teach me Thy way!
Thy guiding grace afford, teach me Thy way!
Help me to walk aright, more by faith, less by sight;
Lead me with heav'nly light, teach me Thy way!

Benjamin lived in England during World War I. Though he was too old to serve in the military during the conflict, his youngest son, Lawrence, did. He was a 30-year-old, unmarried poultry farmer and enlisted in December 1915.

No personal notes have been found about what may have motivated Benjamin Ramsey to write this hymn. However, there may be a "rest of the story" to shed some light on this from an entry on the Roll of Honour website, concerning the West Wittering War Memorial for 1914-1918.

According to this record, Lawrence was a Rifleman for the 5th (City of London) Battalion (Rifle Brigade). While fighting in France on October 9, 1916, he suffered shrapnel wounds to the head and hand from a high explosive shell. He spent three weeks in a hospital and convalescent camp and then was returned to England on a hospital ship on November 6, 1916. Lawrence spent several more weeks in a hospital in England and was discharged from the military on December 28, 1916. Records show that due to his wounds, he was no longer physically fit to serve in the army.

The year in the military was not kind to Lawrence. According to his family, his discharge was on account of his nervous disposition caused by the injury. His hair had turned completely white. He was pale and tremulous, suffering from headaches and dizziness. He slept badly and his memory and concentration were affected. Records in 1918 show that he was living with his brother Wilfred in Surrey. Sadly, he died on

January 7, 1919 at Camberwell House in London—which was a mental hospital.

The hymn "Teach Me Thy Way, O Lord" was written within months of the death of Benjamin Ramsey's son. The final three verses of the hymn, when put into the context of the heartbreaking time for their family, seem very poignant.

When I am sad at heart, teach me Thy way!
When earthly joys depart, teach me Thy way!
In hours of loneliness, in times of dire distress,
In failure or success, teach me Thy way!

When doubts and fears arise, teach me Thy way!
When storms o'erspread the skies, teach me Thy way!
Shine through the cloud and rain, through sorrow,
toil and pain;
Make Thou my pathway plain, teach me Thy way!

Long as my life shall last, teach me Thy way!
Where'er my lot be cast, teach me Thy way!
Until the race is run, until the journey's done,
Until the crown is won, teach me Thy way!

One more clue is left in this story. Ramsey called the melody Camacha, which was a village in Madeira, Portugal. However, it was also the name of the farm of Lawrence Ramsey – a place he left to fight for King and country, and made the ultimate sacrifice for.

Sources:

https://www.conservativewoman.co.uk/the-midweek-hymn-teach-me-thy-way-o-lord/

http://www.roll-of-honour.com/Sussex/WestWittering.html

https://hymnstudiesblog.wordpress.com/2008/11/02/quotteach-me-thy-wayquot/comment-page-1/

FANNY CROSBY

CHAPTER TWELVE

GIVE, OH! GIVE

Have you ever wondered how attitude and perspective make a difference in dealing with the challenges one faces in life? Frances Jane van Alstyne Crosby, more commonly known as Fanny Crosby, focused on what she had, and not what was lacking. To her, finding ways to serve others made all of the difference.

Fanny was born on March 24, 1820 in the village of Brewster, about 50 miles north of New York City, the only child of John and Mercy Crosby. At six-weeks-old, Fanny caught a cold and developed inflammation in her eyes. Because of the advice of the physicians of the day, mustard poultices were applied to treat the discharge. According to Fanny, the procedure damaged her optic nerve, causing her to go blind. When she was six months old, her father died.

She was cared for by her mother and maternal grandmother, both women who had an abiding Christian faith. They realized that though Fanny's eyes were damaged, there was certainly nothing wrong with her mind. They had Fanny memorize long passages from the Bible. From the age of 10, Fanny memorized five chapters of the Bible each week. By the age of 15, she had memorized the four New Testament gospels, the first five books of the Old Testament, the Book of Proverbs, and many of the Psalms.

Fanny also had a talent for composing poetry. A poem which she wrote at the age of nine shows her resolve and disposition to make the best of her life.

> *O what a happy soul am I!*
> *Although I cannot see;*
> *I am resolved that in this world*
> *Contented I will be.*
> *How many blessings I enjoy,*
> *That other people don't;*
> *To weep and sigh because I'm blind,*
> *I cannot and I won't.*

About the age of 12, Fanny attended her first Methodist church services and was delighted by their hymns. This event would later impact her life's work. In 1835, at the age of 15, she became a student at the New York Institution for the Blind, remaining there for eight years as a student and another two years as an instructor. During this time, she learned to play the piano, organ, harp, and guitar and became a good singer. After graduation, she took an active part in lobbying for social causes, including better educational opportunities for people who were blind. She published more than 1,000 secular poems and wrote words to over 60 popular songs.

Then, in 1849, a cholera epidemic raged through New York City. Instead of leaving the city, Fanny stayed at the New York Institute for the Blind to nurse the sick. During this time of sickness and death, Fanny turned her thoughts to the state of her spiritual life and decided something was lacking. Her focus in recent years had not been on religious pursuits, and her relationship with God had been neglected.

Her life moved forward with marriage and the birth of a child, who died shortly after birth. However, her determination to make God a priority in her life continued to grow. Fanny once said:

> "It seemed intended by the blessed providence of God that I should be blind all my life, and I thank him for the dispensation. If perfect earthly sight were offered me tomorrow, I would not accept it. I might not have sung hymns to the praise of God if I had been distracted by the beautiful and interesting things about me."

Fanny used her talents to create lyrics for hymns. Writing more than 8,000 hymns and gospel songs, with more than 100 million printed copies, she was known as the "Queen of Gospel Song Writers" and the "Mother of Modern Congregational Singing in America". Publishers were hesitant to have too many hymns by one person in a hymnal, so she used almost 200 different composer names in her hymns. She once said, "When I get to heaven, the first face that shall ever gladden my sight will be that of my Savior." "A Joyful Song," also called "Behold! A Royal Army," shows her love for Jesus Christ and why her music touched so many. The stirring lyrics she penned were teamed with a lively melody by fellow blind composer, Adam Geibel.

> *Behold! A royal army,*
> *With banner, sword and shield,*
> *Are marching forth to conquer,*
> *On life's great battlefield;*
> *Its ranks are filled with soldiers,*
> *United, bold and strong,*

Who followed their commander,
And sing their joyful song.

Victory, victory,
Through Him that redeemed us!
Victory, victory,
Through Jesus Christ our Lord!
Victory, victory, victory!
Through Jesus Christ our Lord!

In Fanny Crosby's 95 years of life, she was best known as a hymn writer, but also gave her time and money as a rescue mission worker. Fanny could have had a comfortable income, but instead often gave away anything that she did not consider necessary for daily survival. She frequently donated the royalties she earned to worthy causes. During the final three decades of her life, she dedicated her time as "Aunt Fanny" to help at city rescue missions.

Fanny's desire to "give" in the service of others and the Lord, is especially evident in a children's hymn which she wrote— "Give, Said the Little Stream." The lyrics to this song and the simplicity of giving of oneself in the service of others is a message we can all take to heart.

"Give," said the little stream,
"Give, oh! Give, give, oh! give."
"Give," said the little stream,
As it hurried down the hill;
"I'm small, I know, but wherever I go
The fields grow greener still."

"Give," said the little rain,
"Give, oh! Give, give, oh! give."
"Give," said the little rain,
As it fell upon the flowers.
I'll raise their drooping heads again,"
As it fell upon the flowers.

Give, then, as Jesus gives,
Give, oh! give, give, oh! give.
Give, then, as Jesus gives;
There is something all can give.
Do as the streams and blossoms do:
For God and others live.

Chorus:

Singing, singing all the day,
"Give away, oh! give away."
Singing, singing all the day,
"Give, oh! give away."

Fanny Crosby died in 1915 and was buried in a cemetery in Bridgeport, Connecticut, having given her life in the service of others and followed her belief to "give as Jesus gives." Her family erected a very small, simple tombstone at her request, which carried the words: "Aunt Fanny: She hath done what she could."

Sources:

https://www.thetabernaclechoir.org/articles/give-said-the-little-stream.html

https://en.wikipedia.org/wiki/Fanny_Crosby

https://hymnary.org/person/Crosby_Fanny

ELIZA E. HEWITT

CHAPTER THIRTEEN

THE INVALID COMPOSER

Eliza Edmunds Hewitt was born June 28, 1851, the daughter of Captain James Stratton Hewitt and Zeruiah Stites Edmunds Hewitt. She was educated in a girl's normal school in Philadelphia, where she graduated as valedictorian. She took a position teaching school and also served on the staff of the Northern Home for Friendless Children.

The story is told that one day while trying to correct a student, he struck her on the back with the point of a slate, severely injuring her. She was thereafter put in a heavy cast for six months and confined to her bed. Her career was over and for quite some time she was an invalid.

The forced confinement and disappointing circumstances could have made Eliza bitter, but she chose instead to study English literature and to sing sacred songs.

It is said that one warm spring day, after some measure of recovery, she was allowed to go outside and take a walk through Fairmount Park. The blessed sunshine warmed her soul within and without and Eliza returned to her bed and wrote one of her first hymns.

> *There is sunshine in my soul today,*
> *More glorious and bright*
> *Than glows in any earthly sky,*
> *For Jesus is my light.*

Chorus:

Oh, there's sunshine, blessed sunshine
When the peaceful happy moments roll.
When Jesus shows his smiling face,
There is sunshine in the soul.

There is music in my soul today,
A carol to my King,
And Jesus listening can hear
The songs I cannot sing.

There is springtime in my soul today,
For when the Lord is near,
The dove of peace sings in my heart,
The flowers of grace appear.

Eliza Edmunds Hewitt loved the Lord and wrote many songs of glorious praise. It is noteworthy that Eliza, who could have succumbed to pain and bitterness, chose instead to say and feel like the last verse she penned in "There Is Sunshine in My Soul Today."

There is gladness in my soul today,
And hope and praise and love
For blessings which he gives me now,
For joys laid up above.

In a time of stress and challenges, isn't there a powerful lesson and example here for all of us?

Sources:

https://www.hymnologyarchive.com/eliza-hewitthttps://walkerhomeschoolblog.wordpress.com/2015/11/30/the-gospel-songs-of-eliza-edmunds-hewitt/http://littlebirdieblessings.blogspot.com/2012/08/scripture-thursday-sunshine-in-soul.html

CIVILLA D. MARTIN

CHAPTER FOURTEEN

THE SPARROW SONG

The scriptures often provide inspiration for the words to many Christian hymns.

In Matthew 10:29-31 it says, "Are not two sparrows sold for a farthing? And one of them shall not fall on the ground without your Father. But the very hairs of your head are all numbered. Fear ye not therefore, ye are of more value than many sparrows."

Such was the case for this hymn writer.

Civilla Durfee Martin was born in Jordan Falls, Nova Scotia on August 21, 1866, the daughter of James N. and Irene Holden. As an adult, she earned a living teaching school. Civilla met and married Walter Stillman Martin, a Baptist minister, and traveled with him in church work. However, because of somewhat poor health, she remained at home much of the time. She is credited with writing the words to several hundred hymns and religious songs.

Civilla described the circumstances which prompted her to write the words to a certain hymn. She related the following story:

> "Early in the spring of 1905, my husband and I were sojourning in Elmira, New York. We contracted a deep friendship for a couple by the name of Mr. and Mrs. Doolittle—true saints of God. Mrs. Doolittle had been bedridden for nearly twenty

years. Her husband was an incurable cripple who had to propel himself to and from his business in a wheelchair. Despite their afflictions, they lived happy Christian lives, bringing inspiration and comfort to all who knew them. One day while we were visiting with the Doolittles, my husband commented on their bright hopefulness and asked them for the secret of it. Mrs. Doolittle's reply was simple: "'His eye is on the sparrow, and I know He watches me.'"

The woman's simple expression of her faith impressed Civilla and was the catalyst for the words of the hymn that she went home and wrote.

Shortly after writing, she sent the words of the hymn to well-known composer Charles H. Gabriel. In his memoirs he wrote:

"One evening while in a despondent, down-hearted mood, I was glancing over some song-words; none seemed to appeal to me. Presently, I remembered having received a hymn in the day's mail which I had not yet looked at. Taking it from my pocket, it seemed like a voice speaking directly to me as I read, and its melody rang out of silence into my heart exactly as it is sung today. I wrote it out, and in a letter to Mr. Alexander the next day, I mailed it to England where, in Albert Hall, 'The Sparrow Song' was first sung in public."

> *Why should I feel discouraged,*
> *Why should the shadows come,*
> *Why should my heart be lonely,*
> *And long for heaven, heaven and home;*
> *When Jesus is my portion?*
> *My constant Friend is He;*

His eye is on the sparrow,
And I know He watches me.

I sing because I'm happy,
I sing because I'm free;
For His eye, his eye is on the sparrow,
And I know, He watches me.

May we all have faith like Mr. and Mrs. Doolittle to carry on and trust that God's eyes are not just on the sparrow, but also on each of his children.

Sources:

Charles H. Gabriel, Personal Memoirs (1918), p. 41, 46, 47

Charles H. Gabriel, The Singers and Their Songs (Chicago: Rodeheaver, 1916), pp. 52–53: Archive.org

https://www.hymnologyarchive.com/his-eye-is-on-the-sparrow

https://hymnary.org/text/why_should_i_feel_discouraged

DWIGHT L. MOODY

CHAPTER FIFTEEN

THE LOWER LIGHTS

Many ships have been lost at sea, but oceans are not the only place where there are maritime disasters. The Great Lakes, which straddle the United States/Canada border, have had over 8,000 documented shipwrecks. Lake Erie, one of the five lakes, covers 2,000 of them, among the highest concentration of wrecks in the world. The high rocky shore from just east of Cleveland west to Cedar Point combines with shallow water and sudden squalls to create one of the most dangerous stretches of water in the area. This location was likely where a tragic event happened which motivated a writer to pen words for a hymn.

The Rev. Dwight L. Moody, a 19th century evangelist, told a story in one of his sermons of a ship nearing the Lake Erie harbor at Cleveland, Ohio. It was a dark night and a violent storm produced punishing waves. Range lights were used in harbors and consisted of two lights—one higher and set back from the other. When these lights lined up vertically, one exactly above the other, the pilot knew the ship was positioned correctly to navigate the channel. That night, a lighthouse was shining and functioned as the upper range light. The lighthouse keeper's job was to tend to the tall lighthouse, as well as the lower range light lanterns. However, for some reason, that night the lower lights, which were absolutely essential for safe navigation, were not lit.

Seeing only the lights from the lighthouse, the Captain asked the pilot, "Are you sure this is Cleveland?"

"Quite sure," replied the pilot.

"But," said the Captain, "where are the lower lights along the shore?"

"Gone out, sir," replied the pilot.

"Can you make the harbor?" asked the Captain, to which the pilot replied, "we must, sir, or perish."

The pilot steered the vessel on what he thought was a course towards safety. But without the lower lights, he missed the channel. The ship struck upon the rocks and many lives were lost in the cold, stormy Lake Erie water.

Rev. Moody ended his sermon with the admonition, "Brethren, the Master will take care of the great lighthouse; let us keep the lower lights burning."

A young man named Philip P. Bliss heard Rev. Moody's story. He wondered if someone's negligence or misfortune had caused the deadly wreck. Then he questioned if he as a Christian had neglected to do his part. Was he doing enough? Was he an example and reaching out to bring others who may be drowning in sin or misery to a knowledge of Christ? Shortly after the sermon ended, he picked up his pen and began writing both the words and music to "Let the Lower Lights Be Burning."

> *Brightly beams our Father's mercy,*
> *From His lighthouse evermore,*
> *But to us he gives the keeping,*
> *Of the lights along the shore.*

Chorus:

Let the lower lights be burning,
Send a gleam across the way,
Some poor fainting, struggling seaman,
You may rescue, you may save.

Dark the night of sin has settled,
Loud the angry billows roar,
Eager eyes are watching, longing,
For the lights along the shore.

Chorus:

Trim your feeble lamp, my brother,
Some poor sailor, tempest tossed,
Trying now to make the harbor,
In the darkness, may be lost.

Chorus:

The hymn was first published in 1871 in a Sunday School hymnal and became extremely popular. Churches throughout the land began singing this hymn and it blessed millions of people. In the New Testament, Jesus said, "...Inasmuch as ye have done it unto one of the least of these my brethren, ye have done it unto me" (Matthew 25:40). Are you doing all you can to keep the "lower lights" burning to help others?

Sources:

http://plymouthbrethren.org/article/10378

https://iblp.org/sites/default/files/pdf/responsibility_song.pdf

https://www.hymns.com/HYMNS%20OF%20THE%20 MONTH%20PDF/2015%20HYMNS%20OF%20THE%20 MONTH/Brightly-Beams-Our-Father-s-Mercy_February.pdf

http://www.rockthelake.com/buzz/2017/10/lake-erie-hides- secrets-2000-shipwrecks/

THOMAS KEN

CHAPTER SIXTEEN

THE LITTLE CLERIC

Thomas Ken was born in 1637 at Hertfordshire, England. While still a child, he was orphaned and subsequently raised by an older sister. In 1651, young Thomas became a scholar and student at Winchester College. In 1656, he transferred to Oxford University, studying first in Hartford Hall and then in New College. He received his B.A. degree in 1661 and his M.A. in 1664. He served for a time as a tutor in his college. Ken was ordained a minister in 1662, and went out to serve on the Isle of Wight. In 1672, he returned to Winchester College, where he became a "curate in one of the lowest districts." A curate is defined in the Anglican Church as someone charged with the care of souls of a parish.

Thomas Ken is remembered in history for several notable things. First, he loved to sing and write hymns. Second, though a man of small stature, he was known for exceeding faith, courage, and charity. Lastly, he was a powerful and compelling orator and teacher. He cared for the souls of the students at Winchester, so much so in fact, that he combined his love and talents to write *A Manual of Prayers for the Use of the Scholars of Winchester College.*

In 1674, Ken published *A Manual of Prayers for the Use of the Scholars of Winchester College.* "In it, he charged his readers to "be sure to sing the Morning and Evening Hymn in your chamber devoutly, remembering that the Psalmist, upon happy experience, assures you that it is a good thing to tell

of the loving kindness of the Lord early in the morning and of his truth in the night season." Thomas Ken wrote a hymn for his students to sing each morning as they rose. The first verse reads as follows:

> *Awake, my Soul, and with the Sun,*
> *Thy daily Stage of duty run,*
> *Shake off dull Sloath, and joyful rise,*
> *To pay thy Morning Sacrifice.*

> *All Praise to Thee, who safe hast kept,*
> *And hast refresh'd me whilst I slept,*
> *Grant, Lord, when I from Death shall wake,*
> *I may of endless Light partake.*

He wrote another hymn for his students to sing as they ended their day and retired for the night. It reads as follows:

> *All praise to You, my God, this night,*
> *For all the blessings of the light.*
> *Keep me, O keep me, King of kings,*
> *Beneath the shelter of Your wings.*

> *Forgive me, Lord, for this I pray,*
> *The wrong that I have done this day.*
> *May peace with God and neighbor be,*
> *Before I sleep restored to me.*

Lord, may I be at rest in You
And sweetly sleep the whole night thro'
Refresh my strength, for Your own sake,
So I may serve You when I wake.

This little man with the big heart, who cared so deeply for the devotion of his students and their relationship to their God, became known as one of the fathers of English hymnology. You may not know him for his morning and evening hymns, but you will surely know him for the last verse he added to both hymns. It is called "The Doxology," and is sung, like the Christian life of its author, with majesty the world over. It is:

Praise God from whom all Blessings flow,
Praise him all Creatures here below,
Praise him above, ye Heavenly Host.
Praise Father, Son, and Holy Ghost.

Sources:

https://en.wikipedia.org/wiki/Thomas_Ken

https://en.wikipedia.org/wiki/Curate

https://hymnary.org/person/Ken_Thomas

https://kennvillage.co.uk/home-2/history-project/bishop-ken/

https://hymnary.org/text/praise_god_from_whom_all_blessings_ken

COLESHILL, ENGLAND

CHAPTER SEVENTEEN

THE BLIND CARVER

One day in 1842, a visiting Congregational minister, Thomas Salmon, paid a visit to a friend where he lived in Coleshill, Warwickshire, England. Salmon described the visit:

> "I became acquainted with W. W. Walford, the blind preacher, a man of obscure birth and connections and no education, but of strong mind and most retentive memory.
>
> In the pulpit, he never failed to select a lesson well adapted to his subject, giving chapter and verse with unerring precision and scarcely ever misplacing a word in his repetition of the Psalms, every part of the New Testament, the prophecies, and some of the histories, so as to have the reputation of knowing the whole Bible by heart.
>
> He actually sat in the chimney corner, employing his mind in composing a sermon or two for Sabbath delivery, and his hands in cutting, shaping and polishing bones for shoe horns and other little useful implements. At intervals, he attempted poetry.
>
> On one occasion, paying him a visit, he repeated two or three pieces which he had composed, and having no friend at home to commit them to paper, he had laid them up in the storehouse within.

'How will this do?' asked he, as he repeated the following lines, with a complacent smile touched with some light lines of fear lest he subject himself to criticism.

I rapidly copied the lines with my pencil, as he uttered them."

Reverend Salmon left England in 1842 and returned to the United States. In 1845, Salmon submitted an article for the newspaper, The New York Observer, in which he offered the poem composed by William Walford, with this tentative proviso, "if you should think them worthy of preservation."

The editors felt the tender poem worthy of inclusion and published it on September 13, 1845. About fifteen years later, the great composer, William Batchelder Bradbury, set the poem to music. The lovely and touching hymn gained slowly in renown until it was finally published for the first time in 1878 in a Methodist hymnal.

After the hymn was established in the hearts of Christians everywhere, scholars and students went back to find William Walford, the blind poet. They never found him. He remains a mystery yet unsolved. We cannot say for certain who he was or be even the least bit familiar with him, yet the poem he wrote bespeaks a man familiar with His God and the power and intimacy of personal prayer. He wrote:

> *Sweet hour of prayer! Sweet hour of prayer!*
> *That calls me from a world of care,*
> *And bids me at my Father's throne*
> *Make all my wants and wishes known.*
> *In seasons of distress and grief*
> *My soul has often found relief.*

And oft escaped the tempter's snare
By thy return, sweet hour of prayer.

Sources:

https://dianaleaghmatthews.com/sweet-hour-prayer/#.
YH3sfqlKjX0

https://sermonwriter.com/hymn-stories/sweet-hour-prayer/

https://hymnary.org/person/Walford_WW

BRITISH NAVAL SHIP

CHAPTER EIGHTEEN

ALL MERRIMENT
HAD CEASED

In 1923, Dr. J. B. Jeter, in an article entitled *Recollections of a Long Life*, told the story of a man he had met in 1825. He was a Baptist Deacon named Epa Norris, whom he described as "eminently conscientious, fervently devout, and a demonstrative Christian and Baptist. No one could be with him for a few hours without learning something of his religious character and principles."

Dr. Jeter tells that during the war of 1812 between the United States and Great Britain, Deacon Norris, "hearing that the enemy had landed and were marching through the country, he saddled his horse and went forth to make observations and inquiries. He had not gone far when he fell in with a marauding party and was captured as a supposed scout and carried on one of the enemy's vessels lying in the Chesapeake Bay."

Norris was questioned, but refused to tell them anything, saying, "You may kill me, but you cannot make me tell you anything about our army." Subsequently, Norris was kept a prisoner aboard the ship. Perhaps by his courage, he made a favorable impression, but for whatever reason he was invited to the flag ship of the fleet to dine with the ship's officers. There were toasts and songs. At length, Mr. Norris was called on for a song. He modestly declined, but there was a general demonstration of a desire that he should sing. At length, he yielded. He had a fine voice and could sing the familiar

hymns of the day in most plaintive tunes. He struck up in a solemn tune the beautiful Psalm of Isaac Watts:

> *Sweet is the work, my God, my King,*
> *To praise thy name, give thanks, and sing.*
> *To show thy love by morning light,*
> *And talk of all thy truths at night.*

Jeter continued, "The remembrance of his home and family and the pleasant meetings with his brethren, as contrasted with his present captive state, softened his heart and he sung with tearful eyes, these words:

> *Fools never raise their thoughts so high:*
> *Like brutes they live, like brutes they die;*
> *Like grass they flourish, till thy breath*
> *Blast them in everlasting death.*

"Before the old man had finished his Psalm, all merriment had ceased, and a deep solemnity pervaded the festal party. At the close of the singing, the commodore said, 'Mr. Norris, you are a good man, and you shall be sent home.' As soon as arrangements could be made, he bade adieu to the officers, was lowered into a boat, and set ashore with a liberal supply of salt, then very scarce and very valuable in Northern Neck. He soon reached his distressed family with a bosom swelling with gratitude and delight."

Source:

Religious Herald Vol. XCVI. Richmond, VA., November 29, 1923. No. 48

https://books.google.com/books?id=B5fUbWrSPqYC&pg=RA8-PA4&lpg=RA8-PA4&dq=deacon+Epa+Norris&source=bl&ots=4cs4rl56Ug&sig=ACfU3U2ApNQK 2ahUKEwiqoqvekYnxAhXLAZ0JHe3bCJAQ6AE wEHoECBcQAw#v=onepage&q=deacon%20Epa%20 Norris&f=false

KNOWLES SHAW

CHAPTER NINETEEN

THE HARVEST

The Apostle Paul once said, "Whatsoever a man soweth that shall he also reap. For he that soweth to his flesh shall of the flesh reap corruption; but he that soweth to the Spirit shall the Spirit reap life everlasting. And let us not be weary in well doing: for in due season we reap, if we faint not" (Galatians 6:7-9).

The law of the harvest has often been a powerfully personal way of teaching gospel principles to those who live close to the land. For one well known mid-nineteenth century evangelist, the harvest was a metaphor extended to gathering souls to Christ.

Knowles Shaw was born in Butler County, Ohio, on October 13, 1834. His parents, Albin and Huldah Shaw, were both of Scottish descent. The family moved to Rushville, Indiana where Albin was a farmer, stock dealer, and merchant. When Knowles was almost 13, he stood at the bedside of his dying father. Albin gave his son a prized violin and the advice to "Be good to your mother and prepare to meet thy God." Knowles dropped out of school and worked hard to provide for his mother and two sisters. He was a quick learner and acquired many skills through careful observation. One neighbor said that "Knowles Shaw's head was like a tar-bucket, for everything that touched it stuck to it." Albin would have been proud of his son's efforts to care for the

family. However, the second part of his father's advice to be a God-fearing Christian was totally ignored.

Knowles worked diligently to learn to play the violin which his father had given him. In fact, he gained a measure of fame in the area because of his musical skill. He frequently played with bands at dances and parties where alcohol was served. Then one night, while playing his violin at a dance, a most unlikely place for any thought of his eternal welfare, the advice of his father came forcefully and unbidden to his mind—"Prepare to meet thy God!" It seemed to him like a voice from the grave and a message from heaven rested on his soul. The song ended and dancers noisily called for another song.

To the surprise of everyone, Knowles put down the violin and walked to the middle of the floor. He shared with the group his father's dying words and expressed remorse for neglecting religious commitments. He then declared that he would never play violin for another dance and asked the group to not hinder his ability to lead a Christian life. From that hour, Knowles kept that pledge.

He became a faithful church member. For the next two years, Knowles worked as a farm hand, and even married one of his employer's daughters, Martha Finley. However, Knowles felt a call to the harvest of gathering souls to Christ. He worked tirelessly in the churches he was assigned to, having the ability to connect with every social level of people in the communities where he preached.

Knowles Shaw became one of the best-known evangelists in the Restoration Movement. At six feet three inches tall, he was an imposing presence. Because he was an exceptional singer, he was often called the 'Singing Evangelist," integrating hymns into his sermons as part of his message. He was credited with writing over 40 songs which he often sang in revivals. It seems

fitting that the title of one of his final songs, written in 1874 and dedicated to the memory of a fellow preacher, was "Bringing in the Sheaves." Shaw was recognized for bringing thousands of people to a knowledge of Christ, and the words of the song express the zeal he felt in his calling.

Sowing in the morning, sowing seeds of kindness,
Sowing in the noontide and the dewy eve,
Waiting for the harvest and the time of reaping
We shall come rejoicing, bring in the sheaves.

Refrain:

Bringing in the sheaves, bringing in the sheaves,
We shall come rejoicing, bringing in the sheaves.

In May of 1878, Shaw left his wife and family at his home in Columbus, Mississippi to participate in a month of gospel meetings in Dallas, Texas. On June 7, 1878, he answered a call to conduct a revival in McKinney, Texas. While riding there on the train, he was talking to a Methodist minister, Mr. Mallory, when a broken rail caused the train to jump the track. The train car they were in flipped three times before landing in some standing water, forty feet below the tracks. According to Mr. Mallory, Shaw had saved his life by pushing him out of harm's way in the wreck. Twenty-seven people on the train were injured. There was one death—the Singing Evangelist.

According to Mr. Mallory, Knowles Shaw's final words before the accident were, "It is a grand thing to rally people to the Cross of Christ." The final verse of Shaw's hymn seems a fitting

tribute to the young farmer/violinist who committed his life to bringing souls to Christ.

Going forth with weeping, sowing for the Master,
Though the loss sustained our spirit often grieves;
When our weeping's over, He will bid us welcome,
We shall come rejoicing, bring in the sheaves.

Sources:

https://thescottspot.wordpress.com/2016/04/14/bringing-in-the-sheaves-written-in-1874/

https://austinbhebe.wordpress.com/2012/09/27/bringing-in-the-sheave/

https://hymnary.org/person/Shaw_Knowles

https://hymnstudiesblog.wordpress.com/2008/04/14/quotbringing-in-the-sheavesquot/

HENRY FRANCIS LYTE

CHAPTER TWENTY

HENRY FRANCIS LYTE

Henry Francis Lyte was born at Ednam, near Kelso, Scotland in 1793, the second son of Thomas and Anna Maria Lyte. It is believed by some that their marriage was a common law arrangement. When Henry was very young, his father abandoned the family. Shortly after, Henry's mother passed away, leaving him an orphan.

Henry was taken in by the headmaster of his school and raised. In time, Henry went off to the prestigious Trinity College Dublin. While there, he was awarded the English Prize Poem on three occasions. His intention was to study medicine, but instead felt called to the ministry.

Accordingly, he prepared to become an Anglican minister. It was during this formative time that Henry was called to the bedside of a fellow clergyman, William Augustus Le Hunte, who was dying. There was little solace to offer. The man died shortly after. The entire experience was deeply affecting for Henry and he never read the scriptures the same after that, especially as his dying friend had repeatedly pleaded with Henry to "abide with me." It is said by some that Henry was inspired by those words and wrote the first verses of a poem entitled "Abide with Me". The year was 1820.

In 1824, Henry became the minister in Brixham, a coastal fishing village in Devon. The unusually tall, handsome clergyman was an instant draw. So powerful and personal was his charm and style of preaching that it became necessary

to add onto the church to accommodate all who wanted to hear him. Lyte was a man "noted for his wit and human understanding, a born poet and an able scholar. He was an expert flute player and according to his great-grandson, always had his flute with him. Lyte spoke Latin, Greek, and French, enjoyed discussing literature, and was knowledgeable about wildflowers."

Yet, Henry suffered with ill health all his life. Eventually, the chronic weakness of his lungs turned into tuberculosis, yet Henry pressed on as a devoted servant to his people and his family. He was often heard to say, "It is better to wear out than to rust out."

In the 1840's, England was rife with religious dissension. It came home to Henry's parish when a number of his congregants left him, including at one point, his entire choir. That abandonment coupled with his declining health brought him to ponder deeply. It was after this that he wrote a poem in which he voiced the desire to write a hymn that would never die. It reads in part:

"Some simple straw, some spirit-moving lay, some sparkles of the soul that still might live when I was passed to clay...O thou! Whose touch can lend life to the dead, thy quickening grace supply, and grant me, swan like, my last breath to spend in song that may not die!"

Henry's health continued to decline until early September 1847, when he announced to his family that he wanted to preach to his congregation one last time before he went on holiday to Italy. His family protested that the strain would be too much for him. However, he persisted and preached a memorable and magnificent sermon.

That same afternoon, Henry Francis Lyte went for a peaceful walk on the trails that bordered the sea. When he returned home, he retired to his room and a short time later came out and gave to his family the poem that some believe he started in 1820 and finished with meaning in 1847. It was the poem from the heart of a man, terminally ill, in the late evening of life, who had known what it was like to be abandoned—"Abide with Me."

> *Abide with me! Fast falls the eventide;*
> *The darkness deepens. Lord, with me abide!*
> *When other helpers fail and comforts flee,*
> *Help of the helpless, oh, abide with me!*
>
> *Swift to its close ebbs out life's little day.*
> *Earth's joys grow dim; its glories pass away.*
> *Change and decay in all around I see;*
> *O thou who changest not, abide with me!*
>
> *I need thy presence every passing hour.*
> *What but thy grace can foil the tempter's power?*
> *Who, like thyself, my guide and stay can be?*
> *Through cloud and sunshine, Lord, abide with me!*

Henry Francis Lyte died shortly thereafter in 1847. The last words on his lips as he passed were "Peace. Joy!" He never made it to his desired destination of Italy, but he did write the song that would live on and inspire billions.

Sources:

https://anglicancompass.com/the-story-of-our-hymns-abide-with-me-by-henry-francis-lyte/

https://en.wikipedia.org/wiki/Henry_Francis_Lyte

https://www.challies.com/articles/hymn-stories-abide-with-me/

WILL THOMPSON

CHAPTER TWENTY-ONE

WILL THOMPSON: DOING GOOD IS A PLEASURE

William Lamartine Thompson was born on November 7, 1847, in East Liverpool, Ohio. He was the youngest son of seven children. William's father, Josiah Thompson, was a successful businessman and banker, as well as serving for two terms in the Ohio state legislature. His mother, Sarah Jackman Thompson, spent a good deal of time in social and charitable work.

Josiah Thompson had considerable financial success and because of this, his son William had an opportunity for a good education. He improved his already growing musical abilities by attending music schools in Boston and Leipzig, Germany.

It seems that William Thompson watched and learned from his parents' legacy of hard work and service, and this became motivating factors for the rest of his life. When an obstacle was placed in his path, William found a way to move forward.

Writing songs was one of his passions, but the music dealers of the day would not offer him what he thought his songs were worth. Instead of accepting their opinions, William decided to self-publish two secular songs—"My Home on the Old Ohio" and "Gathering Shells from the Seashore." The songs were well received and he earned enough money to open his own music store. By the 1880's, W. L. Thompson Music Company was one of the most successful businesses of that kind in the United States. Thousands of music

teachers and musicians ordered sheet music, instruments, and other supplies from Thompson's store. He founded a music and publishing company in his hometown and Chicago. William also continued to write music and earned the title of the Stephen Foster of Ohio. The man who was discounted by music publishers of the day found his way to move forward and became a millionaire.

At age 44, William married Elizabeth Johnson and they had one son. Because of his financial success, he felt that he owed something to the Lord, so turned his talents to writing only sacred songs. As both a lyricist and composer, Thompson applied his work ethic to the inspiration he often received. He wanted to be sure that he would always remember words or melodies that came to him and kept pencil and paper handy. He said, "No matter where I am, at home or hotel, at the store or traveling, if an idea or theme comes to me that I deem worthy of a song, I jot it down in verse. In this way, I never lose it."

William Thompson's gospel songs were introduced to Christian congregations around the world and translated into many other languages. People in the big cities were able to attend great revivals where his songs were sung. William felt that people in rural communities should hear his music. They did not have the facilities or pianos for concerts. This was an obstacle that William determined to solve. He loaded an upright piano on a two-horse wagon and drove into the country to play and sing his own gospel songs to grateful audiences.

This can-do attitude was exemplified in his hymn "Put Your Shoulder to the Wheel." The expression dates from the 17th century. At that time, the wheels on wooden carts and carriages were large, and big enough to get your shoulder behind. Roads were rutted and muddy and carts often got stuck or overturned. It was necessary to turn the cart upright and push against the

wheels to get unstuck and move forward. It took great effort to accomplish what might seem a formidable task. Pioneers moving across the country were often required to use their strength to push forward. The lyrics are:

> *The world has need of willing men*
> *Who wear the worker's seal.*
> *Come help the good work move along;*
> *Put your shoulder to the wheel.*
> *Put your shoulder to the wheel; push along,*
> *Do your duty with a heart full of song,*
> *We all have work; let no one shirk.*
> *Put your shoulder to the wheel.*

Following in his mother Sarah's footsteps, William contributed to his community. He began the East Liverpool Historical Society and was a trustee of the Carnegie Public Library. In 1899, he donated 100 acres of his own land to the city of East Liverpool for a public park. The gift came with a few restrictions by Thompson. There could be no alcohol or gambling anytime and no ball games on Sundays. His hymn "Have I Done Any Good?" exemplified his feelings about service.

> *Have I done any good in the world today?*
> *Have I helped anyone in need?*
> *Have I cheered up the sad and made someone feel glad?*
> *If not, I have failed indeed.*
> *Has anyone's burden been lighter today*
> *Because I was willing to share?*
> *Have the sick and the weary been helped on their way?*

When they needed my help was I there?
Then wake up and do something more
Than dream of your mansion above.
Doing good is a pleasure, a joy beyond measure,
A blessing of duty and love.

William Thompson was known as a kind, quiet, and unassuming Christian gentleman. He was greatly loved and admired by his associates. His most famous hymn, "Softly and Tenderly Jesus Is Calling" has been printed in 790 hymnals and has been performed and recorded by many famous people.

Softly and tenderly Jesus is calling,
Calling for you and for me;
See, on the portals
He's waiting and watching,
Watching for you and for me.
Come home, come home,
Ye who are weary, come home;
Earnestly, tenderly,
Jesus is calling –
Calling, O sinner, come home!

William Thompson was a personal friend of the famous evangelist D. L. Moody. This hymn was one of his favorites. Moody was very ill and not expected to recover and William paid him a visit. Moody told him, "Will, I would rather have written 'Softly and Tenderly Jesus Is Calling' than anything I have been able to do in my whole life."

William Lamartine Thompson died in 1909, but his legacy of hard work, service, and commitment to spreading the word of God through gospel music continues to inspire the world.

Sources:

https://en.wikipedia.org/wiki/Will_Lamartine_Thompson

http://www.paperlesshymnal.com/tph/Articles/WillThompson.pdf

https://www.phrases.org.uk/meanings/put-your-shoulder-to-the-wheel.html#:~:text=The%20expression%20dates%20from%20the,to%20get%20your%20shoulder%20behind.&text=The%20gist%20of%20the%20story,to%20free%20the%20cart%20himself.

https://www.thetabernaclechoir.org/articles/the-story-behind-softly-and-tenderly.html#:~:text=It%20was%20written%20by%20Will,%2C%20secular%2C%20and%20patriotic%20songs.&text=When%20Moody%20was%20dying%20in,do%20in%20my%20whole%20life.%E2%80%9D

St. Francis of Assissi

CHAPTER TWENTY-TWO

ALL CREATURES OF OUR GOD AND KING

To any and all who recognize the power of Almighty God in His creations, this story is for you.

A baby boy was born to a wealthy silk merchant and his wife in an Italian hill town in 1182 A.D. His mother had him baptized as Giovanni, but when his father returned home from a business trip to France, he started calling him Francesco and had his name changed. Francesco grew up with all of the advantages of the rising merchant class. He learned to read and write and spoke French as well as Italian. Indulged by his parents, Francesco lived a high-spirited life. About 1202, he joined a military expedition fighting as a soldier for his city, and was taken prisoner, spending a year in captivity while also suffering from a severe illness before returning home.

Francesco found that he had lost interest in the pleasures that he once enjoyed. He developed great empathy for the poor and downtrodden. It is said that he had multiple experiences and a vision which persuaded him to devote his life to Christ. He renounced his inherited wealth, and vowed to live a life of poverty and service to God and his fellow man. He took the name Francis of Assisi.

Wearing simple, rough clothes and barefoot, he preached repentance and worked to restore run-down chapels and shrines. He attracted a group of people who led simple lives without possessions. In 1210, he and other followers made a

pilgrimage to Rome and received approval from Pope Innocent III to establish the Franciscan Order of Friars. His band grew and spread across Italy and Mediterranean lands for years, living austere lives and spreading their message of hope and peace.

Surviving manuscripts show that Francis of Assisi was a poet. He felt that people should communicate with God in their own language and not just the Latin language of the church. He is also noted for many quotes which have survived to this day such as:

"If God can work through me, he can work through anyone."

"A single sunbeam is enough to drive away many shadows."

"Lord, make me an instrument of thy peace. Where there is hatred, let me sow love."

Francis of Assisi lived a life close to nature and the wonders of the universe. He called all creatures his "brothers" and "sisters."

It is said that in the year 1226 A.D., St. Francis of Assisi, the man who loved God and His creations with all his soul, lay dying. His last days were spent blind and in terrible pain, lying in an open-air hut in a quiet garden. Notwithstanding his suffering, he gained strength in the garden. The sisters of the nearby convent heard him singing. Francis passed his time in prayer and rejoiced in the peace of the garden. As the end neared, he composed a poem entitled, "The Canticle of the Sun," which was based on Psalm 148. He passed away on the evening of October 3, 1226 singing the Psalms. There are many stories and legends about St. Francis. One of those is that on the moment his spirit took flight, a flock of larks gathered about his little hut and suddenly rose on the wing, singing a beautiful song. On 16 July 1228, he was pronounced a saint by Pope Gregory IX—now revered as St. Francis of Assisi, patron saint of animals and the environment.

Nearly seven hundred years later, at the turn of the twentieth century, William Draper of the Church of England, translated the words of St. Francis to English and set them to music, based on a traditional German melody. Today the text of St. Francis is one of the oldest hymns sung in modern Christianity. The hymn has been published in 246 hymn books.

All creatures of our God and King,
Lift up your voice and with us sing,
Alleluia! Alleluia!
Thou burning sun with golden beam,
Thou silver moon with softer gleam,
Alleluia! Alleluia!

Thou rushing wind that art so strong,
Ye clouds that sail in heav'n along,
Alleluia! Alleluia!
Thou rising morn, in praise rejoice;
Ye light of evening, find a voice,
Alleluia! Alleluia!

Thou flowing water, pure and clear,
Make music for thy Lord to hear,
Alleluia! Alleluia!
Thou fire so masterful and bright,
That gives to man both warmth and light,
Alleluia! Alleluia!

Dear Mother Earth, who day by day
Unfoldest blessings on our way,
Alleluia! Alleluia!

The flow'rs and fruits that in thee grow,
Let them his glory also show,
Alleluia! Alleluia!

Sources:

https://hymnary.org/text/all_creatures_of_our_god_and_king

https://archive.org/details/101hymnstories0000osbe/page/20/mode/2up

https://anglicancompass.com/the-story-of-our-hymns-all-creatures-of-our-god-and-king/

https://www.britannica.com/biography/Saint-Francis-of-Assisi

https://hymnary.org/person/Assisi_F1

SARAH FLOWER

CHAPTER TWENTY-THREE

HE IS A GOD OF HAND

Sarah Flower was born February 22, 1805, the second daughter of Benjamin and Eliza Gould Flower and grew up in a devoutly religious home filled with Bible reading and prayer. Yet, Sarah's father was a friend to all religions and very liberal in his views for the day. Sarah was influenced by a father who once went to prison in defense of his right of free expression and a mother who lost her job as a teacher for refusing to cancel her subscription to a radical newspaper. Sarah was encouraged to accept nothing and question all things. Perhaps such instruction contributed to a crisis of faith she experienced in 1825, at the age of 20. It is recorded of her that she said, "I would give worlds to be a sincere believer, to go to my Bible as I used to, but I cannot."

In 1829, her father passed away. This caused Sarah to sink into a debilitating depression that would last for four years. As time passed, Sarah took up the pen where her father left off, becoming an outspoken champion of the oppressed and an early feminist. She wrote articles, essays, and poems, many of which were political in nature. During that time, her faith was renewed. She did not know all of how or why, but she would write with insight. She said, "It is in the divine spirit of love, swelling in our own hearts, that we must seek and find our God." Sarah learned the great and comforting truth of mortality that God is near us. "He is a God of hand," she wrote, "and not a God afar off."

In 1834, Sarah met and married William Bridges Adams, a widowed engineer and inventor who encouraged Sarah's talents. At his urging she became an accomplished actress, her successful career on stage arrested only by ill health. The lingering effects of tuberculosis that would ultimately end her life at the age of 43, made it impossible for her to maintain the rigors of the stage, and Sarah returned to writing.

By 1840, Sarah had joined a Nonconformist Unitarian Church. It is reported that her minister wanted a new hymn to accompany his next Sunday sermon on Genesis 28:11-19, which is the account of Jacob's ladder where Jacob, on a quest to honor the covenant, has a dream in which he sees a great ladder reaching up to heaven. Jacob sees angels ascending and descending on the ladder. The Lord comes and stands beside Jacob and promises, "I am with thee and will keep thee in all places whither thou goest and will bring thee again into this land; for I will not leave thee, until I have done that which I have spoken to thee of."

Sarah's minister asked her to write a poem to accompany this remarkable passage. After pouring over the scripture, Sarah returned a week later with the poem that her older sister Eliza, a talented composer, set to music. The hymn was performed and loved. Now, more than 180 years later, though some of the words have been altered and there are various tunes to which it is sung, the hymn remains one of the most prized. It is a prayer—a yearning of the soul that God will come and stand beside us—that He will draw us nearer. The hymn is titled "Nearer My God to Thee." These are the words Sarah Flower Adams wrote:

Nearer, my God, to Thee, nearer to Thee!
Even though it be a cross that raiseth me.

Still all my song shall be nearer, my God, to Thee,
Nearer, my God, to Thee, nearer to Thee!

Though like the wanderer, the sun gone down,
Darkness be over me, my rest a stone;
Yet in my dreams I'd be nearer, my God, to Thee,
Nearer, my God, to Thee, nearer to Thee!

There let the way appear steps unto heaven;
All that Thou sendest me, in mercy given;
Angels to beckon me nearer, my God, to Thee,
Nearer, my God, to Thee, nearer to Thee!

Then with my walking thoughts bright with Thy praise,
Out of my stony griefs Bethel I'll raise;
So, by my woes to be nearer, my God, to Thee,
Nearer, my God, to Thee, nearer to Thee!

Or if on joyful wing, cleaving the sky,
Sun, moon, and stars forgot, upwards I fly,
Still all my song shall be, nearer, my God, to Thee,
Nearer, my God, to Thee, nearer to Thee!

Sources:

https://www.thetabernaclechoir.org/articles/nearer-my-god-to-thee-history-and-lyrics.html

https://www.encyclopedia.com/women/encyclopedias-almanacs-transcripts-and-maps/adams-sarah-flower-1805-1848

https://www.christianity.com/church/church-history/timeline/1801-1900/sarah-flower-adams-11630348.html

https://www.oxforddnb.com/view/10.1093/ref:odnb/9780198614128.001.0001/odnb-9780198614128-e-129

https://classicalexburns.com/2019/03/21/sarah-fuller-flower-adams-nearer-my-god-to-thee-the-angelic-dream/

STORMY SEA

CHAPTER TWENTY-FOUR

THIS IS MORE THAN I CAN BEAR

One night, at the Savior's command, the apostles took ship near Capernaum and with Him set out across the Sea of Galilee to the eastern side. Being weary after a long day of teaching, Jesus went to the stern of the boat and was soon asleep on a pillow.

The Sea of Galilee lies several hundred feet below sea level and is prone to extremely high winds coming down off the surrounding hills. This night, an unusually violent storm came down on the lake and the sea rose. Huge waves broke over the small boat, filling it with water until it was on the verge of sinking.

The disciples were experienced fishermen. They knew the lake, yet they were terrified. They fought the storm until all seemed lost. They came to Jesus and awoke Him crying,

"Master, carest thou not that we perish?"

The Savior arose and immediately took in the situation. As the disciples looked on, he stood and rebuked the wind, saying unto the sea, "Peace, be still!" Instantly, the wind abated and there followed a great calm.

Understandably, the disciples were astonished at Him. They knew He had power, but because their fear had overruled their faith, they failed to comprehend how far-reaching His power actually was. They just did not realize what He could actually do.

"What manner of man is this, that even the winds and the sea obey Him, they marveled."

Hundreds of years later, on the other side of the world from the sea of Galilee, the parents of Mary Ann Baker succumbed to the dreaded disease tuberculosis. Now an orphan, Mary Ann went to live with a brother and sister in Chicago. Not long after, it was learned that Mary Ann's brother had the same disease. The two sisters scraped together what means they could and sent their brother to Florida, in hopes that the warmer climate would help him. Mary Ann wrote:

> "He was more than a thousand miles away from home, seeking in the balmy air of the sunny south, the healing that our colder climate could not give. Suddenly, he grew worse. [I] was ill and could not go to him. For two weeks, the long lines of telegraph wires carried back and forth messages between the dying brother and his waiting sisters, ere the word came which told us that our beloved brother was no longer a dweller on the earth. Although we mourned not as those without hope, and although I had believed in Christ [since] early childhood and had always desired to give the Master a consecrated and obedient life, I became wickedly rebellious at this dispensation of divine providence. I said in my heart that God did not care for me or mine.... I have always tried to believe in Christ and give the Master a consecrated life, but this is more than I can bear. What have I done to deserve this? What have I left undone that God should wreak His vengeance upon me in this way?"

But in time, the voice of the Master began to reach even into her troubled heart and peace and calm were born anew.

Not long after, Horatio Richmond Palmer, the choir director and leader in her Chicago Baptist congregation, asked Mary Ann to write a song descriptive of certain stories in the Bible that were being studied in Sunday School. Among those was the story of Jesus calming the sea. Mary Ann said, "The Master's own voice stilled the tempest in my unsanctified heart and brought it to the calm of a deeper faith and a more perfect trust."

From the deep wells of Mary Ann Baker's sacred experience came these words of testimony:

> *Master, the tempest is raging!*
> *The billows are tossing high!*
> *The sky is o'ershadowed with blackness.*
> *No shelter or help is nigh.*
> *Carest thou not that we perish?*
> *How canst thou lie asleep*
> *When each moment so madly is threatening*
> *A grave in the angry deep?*

Chorus:

> *The winds and the waves shall obey Thy will;*
> *Peace, be still! Peace, be still!*
> *Whether the wrath of the storm-tossed sea*
> *Or demons or men or whatever it be,*
> *No waters can swallow the ship where lies*
> *The Master of ocean and earth and skies.*
> *They all shall sweetly obey Thy will.*

Peace, be still! Peace, be still!
They all shall sweetly obey Thy will.
Peace, peace, be still!

Master, with anguish of spirit
I bow in my grief today.
The depths of my sad heart are troubled.
Oh, waken and save, I pray!
Torrents of sin and of anguish
Sweep o'er my sinking soul,
And I perish! I perish! Dear Master.
Oh, hasten and take control!

Chorus:

Master, the terror is over.
The elements sweetly rest.
Earth's sun in the calm lake is mirrored,
And heaven's within my breast.
Linger, Oh, blessed Redeemer!
Leave me alone no more,
And with joy I shall make the blest harbor
And rest on the blissful shore

Chorus:

Sources:

Ernest K. Emurian, Living Stories of Famous Hymns, Boston: W.
A Widdle Co., 1955, pp. 83–85.

https://www.thetabernaclechoir.org/articles/the-history-of-master-the-tempest-is-raging.html

http://www.hymntime.com/tch/htm/m/a/s/t/mastertt.htm

http://www.hymntime.com/tch/bio/p/a/l/m/palmer_hr.htm

https://www.churchofjesuschrist.org/study/general-conference/1984/10/master-the-tempest-is-raging?lang=eng

https://hymnary.org/person/Baker_MaryAnn

Mark 4

JAMES M. BLACK

CHAPTER TWENTY-FIVE

Roll Call

Have you ever wondered about The Book of Life which is written about in the New Testament? Scriptures indicate this is a heavenly record of the faithful, whose names are recorded, as well as an account of their righteous deeds. Thoughts of this book were the catalyst for a popular Christian hymn.

James Milton Black was born in Sullivan County, NY in 1856 to Anna and Nathan Black. In his youth, he received musical training in singing and organ playing in New York and Pennsylvania. In his early twenties, he moved to Williamsport, Pennsylvania where he married and was involved in Christian work through the Mulberry Street Methodist Church. During the week, he would teach music as a song leader, but found his calling in church work as a Sunday School teacher and youth leader. He had a gift for encouraging those with musical and literary abilities and a desire to bring people to a knowledge of the Lord.

James Black had a special affinity for young people and was the president of the church's youth group. One evening, he befriended a poorly dressed teenager who was the daughter of an alcoholic. She lived in a less desirable area of town. He invited her to meetings of the group, but because of her shabby clothes, she hesitated to accept the invitation. Black saw to it that she received appropriate clothes to wear and she became a regular at the youth group gatherings.

One day, he was calling roll at the start of the meeting. Each participant was supposed to recite a scripture verse when his or her name was called, but there was no reply when he said the girl's name. Upon checking, Black found she was very sick with typhoid fever. This was before there were antibiotics, so there was little hope of recovery. Her death came quickly. The fact that she would never again answer to her name at roll call stuck in his mind. He spoke of what a sad thing it would be if your name was called from the Lamb's Book of Life and you were absent.

When Black arrived home, he tried to find a song about a heavenly roll call, but could not find one. He decided to write a song, and the first stanza of the hymn came to his mind, followed soon after by two more verses. Then he sat down at the piano and played the music, note for note, as it is sung to this day. He felt he had been inspired and would never change a single word or note to the hymn. The song "When the Roll Is Called Up Yonder" was sung at the girl's funeral.

When the trumpet of the Lord shall sound, and time shall be no more,
And the morning breaks, eternal, bright and fair;
When the saved of earth shall gather over on the other shore,
And the roll is called up yonder, I'll be there.

When the roll, is called up yonder,
When the roll, is called up yonder,
When the roll, is called up yonder,
When the roll is called up yonder I'll be there.

Many years later, this song comforted a group of distressed children in a Japanese concentration camp. They were at a boarding school in Chefoo, China during the Japanese invasion in 1942 and the students and faculty were forced from their campus and ended up in Weihsien Concentration Camp. This was the same camp that British Olympic Gold Medalist Eric Liddell was sent to.

One evening, about a year before the war ended, some of the older boys were waiting for the evening roll call and as a distraction were jumping and touching a bare wire from the searchlight tower that was hanging low. Some of the boys got shocked, but not seriously injured. A taller boy jumped to touch it and ended up grabbing the wire and bringing it down with him, landing on the damp ground with his bare feet. He was electrocuted.

At the roll call that night, there was no answer when the boy's name was called. At the funeral the following day, an adult leader of the group said that the boy had missed the roll call in camp but had answered one in heaven. The boys and leaders found comfort as they paid tribute to their comrade by singing "When the Roll Is Called Up Yonder." The words to the second verse of the song no doubt had special meaning to the group.

> *On that bright and cloudless morning*
> *When the dead in Christ shall rise,*
> *And the glory of his resurrection share;*
> *When his chosen ones shall gather*
> *To their home beyond the skies,*
> *And the roll is called up yonder, I'll be there.*

Sources:

https://www.lycoming.edu/umarch/image/black/black.pdf

*https://www.christianity.com/church/church-history/
timeline/1801-1900/james-milton-black-wanted-his-name-on-
gods-roll-11630502.html*

*https://en.wikipedia.org/wiki/When_The_Roll_Is_Called_Up_
Yonder*

https://hymnary.org/person/Black_JM

*Morgan, Robert J. (2003). Then Sings My Soul. Thomas Nelson
Publishers, Nashville, p.231.*

GRACE NOLL CROWELL

CHAPTER TWENTY-SIX

Make Me a Poet

Grace Noll was born in Inland Township, Iowa on October 31, 1877, in the middle of a family of seven children. Grace said, "a happier, healthier girl it would have been hard to find."

One of her earliest memories was of her first attempt at writing poetry. Inspired by a lovely scene on her father's farm, she composed a verse and ran in the house to share it with her family, but they laughed at her. She later spoke of that moment:

> "And so that laughter nipped a budding poet, and I never tried to write another line until after I was married. I was a hurt child that day, hurt deeper than even I knew then.... I never tried to write after that until love and romance and a home came to me. That quickened and awakened the desire to write poetry again."

In time, Grace met Norman Crowell, a writer, and because Grace loved words as little girls love dolls, she was smitten. Was she serious when she wrote, "I think he [Norman] could have gone into bank robbing, if he only continued his writing, and I would have seen nothing wrong with him." They were married in 1901. Three years later, their first son was born and Grace loved being a mother and tending a home. "I loved my home and my housekeeping. I was proud of every new article of furniture that entered our door."

But then, Grace was critically injured. Her life became one long series of illnesses and spending months in one hospital after another:

> "It seemed to me at times that all the suffering in the world had been heaped upon my poor back and that I, who so longed to run and play, to tramp the woods, to laugh and sing and shout, would never be able to lift my body again from those hospital beds to take my place, as a normal woman, in the natural walks of life."

As she lay there on those long, sleepless nights, she thought of Robert Louis Stevenson and the asthma that threatened to suffocate him. She reflected on his struggle to survive and concluded:

> "During all those days of suffering and illness, that truly great poet poured himself out in beautiful prose and poetry which, during all the years, has been a source of comfort and joy to little children and to adults. The thing that made Stevenson great was his deep and undying sympathy because he had suffered."

Grace prayed that some good might come of her suffering and for the first time since the age of eight, she ventured to write a little poem called "A Prayer for Courage." The poem was sent out and immediately, she said, "the letters began to come back to me from fellow sufferers."

The response she received heartened her and gave her courage and vision. She said:

> "To think that I, a nerve-wracked, pain-ridden mother, who found caring for a little child a task almost too much for her daily strength, whose hours were being spent in bed or on a couch, could do a

thing like that, was almost unthinkable. The thought kept coming to me, "I would like to write poetry that will help others who are suffering as I am." My English education had been almost negligible; I had never pictured myself as a serious writer. And yet, I found myself praying to God… to make me a poet, a real poet, one of the best, and promising to honor Him in whatever I wrote, if only He gave me words to say."

Her prayers were answered, and the poems came, to the delight of a welcoming world. Over the decades that followed, Grace wrote more than 5,000 poems, published in 35 volumes. She became in her time, "the most popular writer of verse in America." In 1935, she was named Poet Laureate of Texas. Dale Carnegie called her "one of the most beloved poets in America." So overwhelming was the response to her poetry, that her husband quit his job just to manage the correspondence.

All of this happened from a bed of affliction. Grace yearned to go out and help people, but lacked the strength to do so.

"Sorrow and suffering," she said, "are universal experiences, and it is out of suffering that I have written just my own experiences, reactions and hopes, and they seem to have found a response in other hearts. I have tried to find the silver lining to every dark cloud, both for myself and for all who have suffered."

It is profoundly significant, therefore, that it was Grace Noll Crowell who wrote these words:

Because I have been given much, I too must give;
Because of thy great bounty, Lord, each day I live.

I shall divide my gifts from thee
With every brother that I see
Who has the need of help from me.

Sources:

https://ccdesan.livejournal.com/138303.html

https://allpoetry.com/Grace-Noll-Crowell

https://www.hometownsource.com/sun_thisweek/a-look-at-the-past-farmington-woman-wrote-over-5-000-poems/article_56d15a92-43f4-11e8-80e9-6f90f8f297d6.html

http://www.fbchsv2.org/blindfaith/2013/11/13/because-i-have-been-given-much/

https://www.tshaonline.org/handbook/entries/crowell-grace-noll

PHILLIP DODDRIDGE

CHAPTER TWENTY-SEVEN

HOW GENTLE

Have you ever known someone who is a genuine peacemaker? In Matthew 5:9 it says, "Blessed are the peacemakers: for they shall be called the children of God." Over 300 years ago, there was a noble soul who tried very hard to do just that.

Philip Doddridge was born in 1702 in London, England. His father was a prosperous businessman. Phillip's first lessons came from his mother, who taught him Bible stories which were depicted on the Dutch tiles decorating the chimney of their home. Both of his grandfathers were ministers, though they died before he was born. It is likely that their legacy influenced him.

Philip's paternal grandfather was part of the clergy of the Church of England. In 1662, during the reign of Charles II, an "Act of Uniformity" was passed by Parliament, setting out how services in the Church of England were to be conducted and prescribing the use of a certain edition of the "Book of Common Prayer." The clergy were required to publicly declare their approval or lose their positions. His grandfather stood against the King of England in defense of his principles and was ejected from the Church, one of many who left and endured the restrictions imposed on dissenters. He became a pastor of a Nonconformist church.

In 1626, Philip's maternal grandfather lived in the city of Prague. Emperor Ferdinand II attempted to force Catholicism on all of his subjects. As a Lutheran minister, he was forced

to flee Prague because of religious persecution. He came to England and established a grammar school in greater London.

Philip was the youngest of twenty children. His mother died when he was eight years old. At the age of thirteen, his father died and Philip became an orphan. Only one of his siblings, a sister, survived to adulthood.

In spite of these hardships, he attended school, first studying law and then deciding to train for the ministry. The Duchess of Bedford offered to finance his university education at Oxford or Cambridge to prepare for a position in the Church of England. Like his grandfathers, he declined, refusing to consent to conform and choosing instead to retain his independence. His faith, which had come at his mother's knee, undoubtedly taught him to cherish the principles of his fathers.

In 1730, he married a young lady named Mercy. They had nine children, with four living to adulthood, and the family enjoyed a happy home life together.

In due course, Philip became a Presbyterian minister at a time and in a place of religious contention. Yet, having seen enough of intolerance and bigotry, Philip sought tirelessly for healing and unity. One biographer said this of him, "Doddridge carried out his own ideal with great fidelity and with conspicuous success, doing more than any man in the 18th century to obliterate old party lines, and to unite nonconformists on a common religious ground."

Moreover, Doddridge cared for the poor, no matter their religious persuasions:

> "He set up a charity school for teaching and clothing the children of the poor…. He had an important share in the foundation of the county infirmary. He proposed the formation of a society for distributing

bibles and other good books among the poor. His scheme for the advancement of the gospel at home and abroad, presented to three different assemblies of ministers in 1741, has been described as the first nonconformist project of foreign missions.... In 1748, he laid before Archbishop Herring a proposal for occasional interchange of pulpits between the established and dissenting clergy."

As a peacemaker, he believed that all denominations as true Christians should work together.

In addition to his duties as a Congregationalist minister, he managed a theological academy which trained 200 young men to be ministers in Nonconformist churches. He had the reputation of making every minute of the day count. He wrote 400 hymns, most to accompany his sermons, and was a friend and admirer of hymn writer Isaac Watts.

Philip Doddridge was a model of how Christians should live. Because of his life experiences, he was able to look on others with love, no matter their circumstances or beliefs. The effects of tuberculosis ended his life at the age of 49. To his highest honor, Doddridge's daughter said of him, "The orthodoxy my father taught his children was charity." One of the many hymns he wrote, "How Gentle God's Commands," was a testament to this gentle man and his beliefs.

> *How gentle God's commands!*
> *How kind his precepts are!*
> *Come, cast your burdens on the Lord*
> *And trust his constant care.*

Beneath his watchful eye,
His Saints securely dwell;
That hand which bears all nature up
Shall guard his children well.

Why should this anxious load
Press down your weary mind?
Haste to your Heav'nly Father's throne
And sweet refreshment find.

His goodness stands approved,
Unchanged from day to day;
I'll drop my burden at his feet
And bear a song away.

In an age and time, much like our own, when the love of men waxes cold, Philip K. Doddridge was a rare soul and peacemaker who understood this eternal truth—that God is a loving, gentle Father who desires His children to take care of one another, and treat each other with love and tolerance.

Sources:

https://en.wikisource.org/wiki/Dictionary_of_National_Biography,_1885-1900/Doddridge,_Philip

http://www.laricemusic.com/2014howgentlegodscommands.html

https://hymnary.org/text/how_gentle_gods_commands

James Montgomery

CHAPTER TWENTY-EIGHT

The Stranger

James Montgomery was born on November 4, 1771, in Irvine, Scotland, the son of a minister. At the age of six, James was sent to school near Leeds, England. His two brothers came in later years. In 1783, the family spent three months together before his parents departed for the West Indies as missionaries. James would never see them again, as they died in the mission field. He would later say of them, "They made the first deep furrows with the gospel plough and fell down dead in them through excessive labor."

While a student there, James came to love poetry. Though such was forbidden at the school, he "frequently found means to borrow books and read by stealth." It became a passion to write poetry, albeit one that distracted from his prescribed studies. By the age of thirteen, he had filled his first volume. He was excelling as a poet and writer, but not as a student. Consequently, he was put to work out of the school as a store clerk. At age 16, he "determined to break loose and see the world." He found employment of his own choosing and devoted his leisure time to reading and composing poetry.

In April 1792, James answered an ad for a bookkeeper at a newspaper called *The Sheffield Register*. Politics and divisive issues were the hot fodder of newspaper print for the time, and James found himself drawn in. "I entered in the feelings of those who avowed themselves the friends of freedom, justice, and humanity," he later wrote. Because the paper was political

in its views, Editor Gale, James' employer, became a target for the opposition and was forced to flee to America. James took over the editorship and renamed the paper the *Sheffield Iris*. In the first issue, James published the paper's lofty motto, "Ours are the plans of fair, delightful, peace, unwarped by party rage, to live like brothers." But peace it was not to be. Within two months, James was served with a warrant, convicted, and sentenced to three months imprisonment in York Castle on false charges of sedition. His paper had done a favor for a man in printing a song that was deemed seditious. James neither approved it, nor set the type, but he served the time. He was released, but in the routine reporting of a politically-charged riot in Sheffield, he once again found himself crosswise with King and magistrate. This time, James was unjustly sentenced to six months in the Castle at York. He bore his punishment with meekness and while his health declined, his conscience remained bright.

Upon returning to his editorial duties, he continued to write:

> "He gave unstintingly of his literary talent for the support of worthwhile religious and humanitarian causes. He became recognized as the friend of the people…. as a champion of the cause of liberty and freedom. He interceded in behalf of slaves, the chimney sweeps, widows, and the destitute."

To the end of his days, James served his fellowman with deeds of philanthropy, championing worthy causes, the composing of hymns, and the publishing of poems. In 1849, the now-celebrated poet and composer became seriously ill and while listening to some of his own hymns commented:

> "As all my hymns embody some portion of the history of the joys and sorrows, the hopes and fears of this poor heart, so I cannot doubt but they will be found

an accurate vehicle of expression for the experience of many of my fellow-creatures who may be similarly exercised during the pilgrimage of the Christian life."

On Sunday, April 30, 1854, James Montgomery passed away quietly in his sleep. "The forges and workshops of smoky Sheffield were deserted for the public funeral. Thousands of mourners swelled the funeral train which took an hour to pass any given point. The common man had lost an uncommon friend."

James Montgomery, patriot, poet, and friend of God and man wasted and wore out his life in service to all. He spoke with hope that his words would give expression to others who shared "similar experiences in the pilgrimage of the Christian life." Those hopes would be fulfilled beyond anything he could have possibly imagined. James became one of Britain's greatest poets and composers. You may not recognize all that he wrote, but you will surely rejoice at a poem he wrote in 1826 that he titled, "The Stranger." The poem was surely autobiographical of the life of James Montgomery. It begins thus:

> *A poor, wayfaring Man of grief*
> *Hath often crossed me on my way,*
> *Who sued so humbly for relief*
> *That I could never answer nay.*
> *I had not power to ask his name,*
> *Whereto he went, or whence he came;*
> *Yet there was something in his eye*
> *That won my love; I knew not why.*
>
> *Once, when my scanty meal was spread,*
> *He entered; not a word he spake,*

Just perishing for want of bread.
I gave him all; he blessed it, brake,
And ate, but gave me part again.
Mine was an angel's portion then,
For while I fed with eager haste,
The crust was manna to my taste.

I spied him where a fountain burst
Clear from the rock; his strength was gone.
The heedless water mocked his thirst;
He heard it, saw it hurrying on.
I ran and raised the sufferer up;
Thrice from the stream he drained my cup,
Dipped and returned it running o'er;
I drank and never thirsted more.

'Twas night; the floods were out; it blew
A winter hurricane aloof.
I heard his voice abroad and flew
To bid him welcome to my roof.
I warmed and clothed and cheered my guest
And laid him on my couch to rest,
Then made the earth my bed and seemed
In Eden's garden while I dreamed.

Stripped, wounded, beaten nigh to death,
I found him by the highway side.
I roused his pulse, brought back his breath,
Revived his spirit, and supplied
Wine, oil, refreshment—he was healed.
I had myself a wound concealed,

But from that hour forgot the smart,
And peace bound up my broken heart.

In prison I saw him next, condemned
To meet a traitor's doom at morn.
The tide of lying tongues I stemmed,
And honored him 'mid shame and scorn.
My friendship's utmost zeal to try,
He asked if I for him would die.
The flesh was weak; my blood ran chill,
But my free spirit cried, "I will!"

Then in a moment to my view
The stranger started from disguise.
The tokens in his hands I knew;
The Savior stood before mine eyes.
He spake, and my poor name he named,
"Of me thou hast not been ashamed.
These deeds shall thy memorial be;
Fear not, thou didst them unto me."

That poem would later be set to music by George Coles and retitled. We know it today as "A Poor Wayfaring Man of Grief."

Sources:

Information and quotations for this story comes from a Master's Thesis written in May 1950 by Robert Williamson and titled, The Religious Thought of James Montgomery. https://era.ed.ac.uk/bitstream/handle/1842/10190/0074214c.pdf

KATHARINE LEE BATES

CHAPTER TWENTY-NINE

Pikes Peak

It was the summer of 1893 when Katharine Lee Bates, Professor of Literature at Wellesley College in Massachusetts, set out for Boulder, Colorado to teach summer courses at Colorado College. Along the way, she stopped in Chicago to visit the World's Fair. She was particularly impressed by the displays of the fair and its hope for the future, particularly the "White City."

She continued on across Kansas, and arrived at her destination. Katharine later shared the following:

> "One day, some of the other teachers and I decided to go on a trip to 14,000-foot Pikes Peak. We hired a prairie wagon. Near the top, we had to leave the wagon and go the rest of the way on mules. I was very tired. But when I saw the view, I felt great joy. All the wonder of America seemed displayed there, with the sea-like expanse.
>
> It was then and there, as I was looking out over the sea-like expanse of fertile country spreading away so far under those ample skies, that the opening lines of the hymn floated into my mind. When we left Colorado Springs, the four stanzas were penciled in my notebook, together with other memoranda, in verse and prose, of the trip. The Wellesley work soon absorbed time and attention again, the notebook was laid aside, and I do not

remember paying heed to these verses until the second summer following, when I copied them out and sent them to The Congregationalist, where they first appeared in print July 4, 1895. The hymn attracted an unexpected amount of attention. It was almost at once set to music by Silas G. Pratt. Other tunes were written for words and so many requests came to me, with still increasing frequency, that in 1904 I rewrote it, trying to make the phraseology more simple and direct."

Katharine was paid five dollars for the first sale of her poem. Then, in a remarkable turn of events, someone took a tune written by Samuel Ward, titled "Marterna," and married it to Katharine's poem. Samuel Ward and Katharine Lee Bates never met, but out of their inspired genius came a hymn that has moved the hearts of millions in love for America. Those words are:

> *Oh, beautiful for spacious skies,*
> *For amber waves of grain*
> *For purple mountain majesties*
> *Above the fruited plain!*
> *America! America! God shed his grace on thee,*
> *And crown they good with brotherhood*
> *From sea to shining sea.*
>
> *Oh, beautiful for pilgrim feet,*
> *Whose stern, impassioned stress*
> *A thoroughfare of freedom beat*
> *Across the wilderness!*
> *America! America! God mend thine ev'ry flaw,*

Confirm thy soul in self-control,
Thy liberty in law.

Oh, beautiful for heroes proved
In liberating strife,
Who more than self their country loved,
And mercy more than life!
America! America! May God thy gold refine,
Till all success be nobleness,
And ev'ry gain divine.

Oh, beautiful for patriot dream
That sees beyond the years
Thine alabaster cities gleam,
Undimmed by human tears!
America! America! God shed his grace on thee,
And crown thy good with brotherhood
From sea to shining sea.

It was in 1931 that "The Star-Spangled Banner" was voted by Congress as America's National Anthem. There were many then and since who felt that "America the Beautiful" with its faith, prayer, and hopes for brotherhood is more fitting as a national anthem.

Speaking of the success of her poem, Katharine Lee Bates said:

> "That the hymn has gained, in these twenty odd years, such a hold as it has upon our people, is clearly due to the fact that Americans are at heart idealists, with a fundamental faith in human brotherhood."

Source:

https://www.classicchicagomagazine.com/america-the-beautiful-the-chicago-connection/

https://americanliterature.com/author/katharine-lee-bates

https://www.songhall.org/profile/Katharine_Lee_Bates

PHILLIP PAUL BLISS

CHAPTER THIRTY

THE MAN WHO WANTED MORE

The dictionary defines the word more as a greater or additional amount of something. The desire to learn and give more was important in the life of an American hymnist and composer.

Phillip Paul Bliss was the third child born to Isaac and Lydia Doolittle Bliss in July of 1838. The family lived in a log cabin on a homestead in a rural Appalachian mountain region of northern Pennsylvania. His father was of Welsh descent and a devout Christian who was always singing gospel songs. Young Phillip learned to sing with his father and to play on reeds or other simple musical instruments which he made himself. From an early age, Phillip loved music. His family was very poor and opportunities to go to school were limited, but his mother taught him to read from the Bible.

When Phillip was 10 years old, he was selling vegetables to people in the community to help support his family. He first saw a piano in one of the homes —and Phillip wanted to learn more about this fascinating instrument. Barefoot and ragged, he went uninvited through an open door into the parlor. He stood mesmerized until the music stopped and then said, "O lady, play some more." He was quickly sent out of the home, but the experience introduced him to a whole new world of music.

At the age of eleven, Phillip left home to work on a farm, carrying all of his clothing done up in a handkerchief. For the next five years he worked on farms and in lumber

camps, taking every opportunity for schooling. Finally, at the age of seventeen, Phillip was able to fulfill his desire for more learning and went to school in East Troy, Pennsylvania, where he completed his teaching credentials and taught school the winter of 1856. Not forgetting his love of music, the following year he spent the winter receiving his first formal instruction in music at a singing school. He had a wonderful bass voice. In 1859, he married the love of his life, Lucy Young. They lived with Lucy's father in Rome on the Susquehanna River, helping him farm. Teaching music lessons in the evenings gave Phillip an even greater desire to learn more about music.

A pivotal moment came in his life in 1860 when he heard of a Normal Academy of Music which would be held 125 miles northwest in Geneseo, New York. Some of the most notable musicians of the region would be teaching a six-week training course for music teachers—but it cost the huge sum of thirty dollars and there was no way the young couple could afford the fee. His wife's Grandma Allen saw how heartbroken Phillip was and told him that thirty dollars was indeed a good deal of money. Then the dear lady produced an old stocking which she had been dropping pieces of silver in for years. There was more than the amount he needed and she donated her money so that Phillip could realize his dream to learn more about music. Over the next five years, he became financially successful, saving enough money to purchase a small cottage in Rome and move his parents from their humble backwoods home to live with them.

Phillip had one successful singing concert tour in Chicago. Shortly after, he was drafted into the Union Army at the end of the Civil War, where he served for a few weeks and was honorably discharged. After sending a manuscript of music he had written to Root and Cady Musical Publishers, he was hired and worked there from 1865-1873 conducting musical conventions, singing schools, and concerts for his employers.

He wrote and published several hymns. Some would say that the dreams of a poor 10-year-old boy who wanted more were realized.

However, as time went on, Phillip Bliss began searching for something more in his life. In 1869, he became acquainted with evangelist Dwight L. Moody and went to many of his meetings. Phillip became acquainted with Horatio Spafford, writing the music to his text for the hymn "It Is Well with My Soul." Moody and Horatio Spafford both urged him to give up his job and become a missionary singer. In 1873, he entered into full time missionary work. After committing himself and all his gifts to the Lord's service, he wrote one of his greatest hymns which he called "My Prayer." The hymn became a favorite of Mr. Moody and Phillip Bliss was often called upon to sing it in their meetings. The pastor of the First Congregational Church of Chicago, of which Phillip was a member, told the following story:

> "He came in late one evening and sat at the rear of the church. Seeing him, I called him forward to sing the hymn, 'My Prayer.' He struck the keys on the piano, stooped forward, and reading the words in the latter part of the first verse, more joy in his service, said I do not think I can sing that as a prayer anymore; it seems to me that I have as much joy in serving the blessed Master as it is possible for me to bear."

Bliss and his wife, Lucy, met a tragic end while on the way to a revival, losing their lives in the Ashtabula River railway disaster in Ohio on December 29, 1876. A trestle bridge collapsed, sending the train cars plummeting into the ravine and causing some to catch fire.

Philip P. Bliss, the man who wanted more, said this before his passing:

"Thus the overruling Providence has led me by unmistakable evidence to see and recognize His dealing with me all through life's journey. Truly we have much to be thankful for. My dear wife, my greatest earthly treasure, joins in the opinion that we are and ever have been highly favored of Heaven; that we find our greatest enjoyment in each other's society, when striving to make each other happy, and our highest aim is to be useful to ourselves and others, and to glorify God that we may enjoy Him forever."

Millions of Christians have made this song their prayer as well, seeking for more of what is most important in life.

More holiness give me,
More strivings within,
More patience in suffering,
More sorrow for sin,
More faith in my Savior,
More sense of his care,
More joy in his service,
More purpose in prayer.

More gratitude give me,
More trust in the Lord,
More pride in his glory,
More hope in his word,
More tears for his sorrows,
More pain at his grief,
More meekness in trial,
More praise for relief.

More purity give me,
More strength to o'ercome,
More freedom from earth stains,
More longing for home.
More fit for the kingdom,
More used would I be,
More blessed and holy –
More, Savior, like thee.

Sources:

http://www.hymntime.com/tch/htm/m/o/r/e/h/moreholi.htm

https://www.thetabernaclechoir.org/articles/more-holiness-give-me.html

https://www.hymns.com/HYMNS%20OF%20THE%20MONTH%20PDF/2015%20HYMNS%20OF%20THE%20MONTH/Brightly-Beams-Our-Father-s-Mercy_February.pdf

https://www.wholesomewords.org/biography/biobliss.html

ANNIE SHERWOOD HAWKS

CHAPTER THIRTY-ONE

ANNIE SHERWOOD HAWKS

Annie Sherwood Hawks was a thirty-seven-year-old mother of three children. She held no positions of authority or prominence as the world might see it. In fact, she never graduated from any schools. No, she was a homemaker and a mom living in Brooklyn, New York. She had loved and composed poetry since she was a child and as the years passed, many of her works were published. With that meaningful background, Annie tells how a most significant piece of poetry came to her:

> "One day as a young wife and mother of 37 years of age, I was busy with my regular household tasks during a bright June morning [in 1872]. Suddenly, I became so filled with the sense of nearness to the Master that, wondering how one could live without Him, either in joy or pain, these words were ushered into my mind, the thought at once taking full possession of me—'I Need Thee Every Hour.'"

> *I need thee every hour,*
> *Most gracious Lord.*
> *No tender voice like thine*
> *Can peace afford.*
> *I need thee, oh, I need thee;*
> *Every hour I need thee!*

Oh, bless me now, my Savior;
I come to thee.

As the words flowed into her mind, Annie sat down at a desk by the open window and wrote the lines of the poem. In her mind, it was a poem and a prayer that expressed the fullest feelings of her heart.

Sometime after, she took the poem and showed it to Pastor Robert Lowry, who himself was an accomplished writer and composer. Dr. Lowry added the chorus and composed a simple melody. The hymn immediately caught on, becoming popular on both sides of the Atlantic Ocean. By the time of her death in 1918, "I Need Thee Every Hour" had been translated into more languages than any other Christian hymn.

Annie marveled appreciatively at the popularity and power of her hymn to touch people's lives—not fully comprehending it herself. That is, until 1888, when the words and power of her own hymn finally echoed back to her. Annie's husband, Charles Hawks, died. She wrote:

> "I did not understand at first why this hymn had touched the great throbbing heart of humanity. It was not until long after, when the shadow fell over my way, the shadow of a great loss, that I understood something of the comforting power in the words which I had been permitted to give out to others in my hour of sweet serenity and peace. Now when I hear them sung, as I have sometimes, by hundreds of voices in chorus, I find it difficult to think they were ever, consciously, my own thoughts or penned by my own hand."

When one has sung all five of the verses, they will have proclaimed with heart and voice 20 times, "I Need Thee."

Sources:

https://www.umcdiscipleship.org/resources/history-of-hymns-i-need-thee-every-hour

https://www.hymnologyarchive.com/i-need-thee-every-hour

https://en.wikipedia.org/wiki/Annie_Hawks

ISAAC WATTS

CHAPTER THIRTY-TWO

GIVE US SOMETHING BETTER

Isaac was a young man who had a first-hand knowledge of intolerance. Born in 1674, he was the first child of a committed religious Dissenter/Nonconformist, who was a deacon of the Independent or Congregational Church in England. His father was imprisoned twice for his views which did not align with the religion practiced by the reigning monarchy. As a baby, his mother would nurse him on the prison steps and hold Isaac up to the window for his father to see.

Isaac's father ran a boarding school of high repute, and students were sent not only from England, but as far away as America and the West Indies to live and study. Young Isaac attended classes in school and early on showed a precocious intellect. At age four, he began to learn Latin, and by the age of thirteen he had added Greek, French, and Hebrew to his studies.

His intelligence was recognized by a local physician and other prosperous donors in the community and they offered to sponsor him to attend university at Oxford or Cambridge. A youth with so much promise deserved an education in the best schools in the country – however, because of prejudice and intolerance, he could not attend unless he renounced his family's Nonconformist beliefs. Instead, he chose to be educated at the Dissenting Academy in Stoke Newington, London.

Leaving the Academy at the age of 20, Isaac spent two years at home. One of his driving concerns was the poor quality of congregational singing in the churches he attended. The worshippers were restricted to texts of strict metrical versions of the Psalms from the Old Testament. The congregants sang slowly and without heart. One Sunday, after complaining about the singing in the church service, his father challenged, "Why don't you give us something better to sing?" Isaac accepted his father's challenge.

We know Isaac today as Isaac Watts, and he revolutionized the music sung by the Christian world. Having a talent for writing and producing rhyming poems in daily conversation, he wrote a new song each week for two years, which were enthusiastically sung by the congregation where his family attended church. He published these in a book titled *Hymns and Spiritual Songs* in 1709. During his lifetime, he wrote the words for over 800 hymns, but most were written during these two golden years. Some texts were based on psalms, while others were not straightforward translations. When critics criticized his efforts saying it was not right to sing uninspired hymns not taken exactly from the Psalms, he replied that if people could pray to God in sentences that they made up themselves, then surely, they could sing to God in the same way.

In 1702, he became the pastor of the Independent Church, Berry Street, London, a position which he held for ten years. One friend who knew him wrote:

> "He measured only about five feet in height, and was of a slender form. His complexion was pale and fair, his eyes small and gray, but animated, became piercing and expressive; his forehead was low and his cheekbones prominent. His voice was pleasant, but weak. A stranger would probably have been most

attracted by his piercing eye, whose very glance was able to command attention and awe."

Once at a hotel with some friends, Isaac overheard a rude remark from someone in the room who said, "What! Is that the great Dr. Watts?" His reply to his critic was:

"Were I so tall to reach the pole,
Or grasp the ocean with my span,
I must be measured by my soul,
The mind's the standard of the man."

Because of poor health and severe illness in 1712, he went to the house of Sir Thomas Abney to convalesce for a week, and stayed at their residence for the next 36 years as their guest. He wrote extensively, including a legacy of hymns, educational works, sermons, and essays.

Religious intolerance continued to be a part of Isaac's life. Dissenters in the empire were treated very badly. During the reign of Queen Anne in England in 1714, she forced through Parliament the Schism Act, which had the aim of severely limiting religious freedoms. The Act was meant to constrain, convert, or stop Dissenter schools.

It was at this turbulent time that Isaac Watts wrote the lyrics to a song which he hoped would impart assurance and courage to those standing with him on religious principle. It was a paraphrase of Psalm 90:1-5. Today that hymn, which was written in conflict, has spanned the world and been published in 1,149 hymnals.

O God, our help in ages past,
Our hope for years to come,
Our shelter from the stormy blast,
And our eternal home.
 Beneath the shadow of thy throne,
Thy saints have dwelt secure;
Sufficient is thine arm alone,
And our defense is sure.

Before the hills in order stood,
Or earth received her frame,
From everlasting thou art God,
To endless years the same.

A thousand ages in thy sight
Are like an evening gone;
Short as the watch that ends the night
Before the rising sun.

Time, like an ever-rolling stream,
Bears all its sons away;
They fly, forgotten, as a dream
Dies at the opening day.

O God, our help in ages past,
Our hope for years to come,
Be thou our guide while life shall last,
And our eternal home.

Isaac Watts died in November 1748 in his 75th year. Monuments were erected in his hometown of Southampton, as well as in the Church of England's Westminster Abbey, in recognition of his contributions to church music. To this day, some 300 years later, he is known as the Father of English Hymnody, not only for what he wrote, but because he freed the hearts of the people to pray and worship by song.

Sources:

https://books.google.com/books?id=X-wWAAAAYAAJ&pg=PA1 55&lpg=PA155&dq=Deacon+Epa+Norriss%2Bwar+of+1812 %2BSweet+is+the+work+my+god+my+king&source=bl&ots= UIHeTdKdTK&sig=ACfU3U0uOpguoyT68K8yTO-gE0_5_ UdbbA&hl=en&sa=X&ved=2ahUKEwj4_ZayoubwAhWTW8 0KHfcsA7oQ6AEwEnoECAkQAw#v=onepage&q=Deacon%20 Epa%20Norriss%2Bwar%20of%201812%2BSweet%20is%20 the%20work%20my%20god%20my%20king&f=false

https://hymnary.org/person/Watts_Isaac

http://justus.anglican.org/resources/bio/70.html

https://www.google.com/search?q=o+god+our+help+in+ages+past+lyrics &rlz=1C5CHFA_enUS720US720&oq=o&aqs=chrome.0.69i59j69i57j 35i39l2j46i199i291i433i512j0i512j46i199i291i433i512j0i131i433i 512l2j0i512.2778j0j15&sourceid=chrome&ie=UTF-8

Thomas Rawson Taylor

CHAPTER THIRTY-THREE

THOMAS RAWSON TAYLOR

Thomas Rawson Taylor was born May 9, 1807, at Ossett, near Wakefield, England, the son of the Rev. Thomas Taylor. When he came of age, he pursued the occupation of a merchant and then a printer, but a desire to serve God overwhelmed all else. At the age of 18, he began to study for the ministry. On one occasion, while passing through the village of Sheffield, he was invited to preach at a local chapel. He preached a sermon titled, "To the Young", which was so well received that he was invited back again and again. It was hoped by the congregants that the young man would become their pastor. He was appointed in July 1830.

Immediately, the young man distinguished himself, not only for his articulate ability to preach and connect with his people, but also for his love and devotion to those he served. He was there in their hour of need. In December 1830, he stood before his congregation and reportedly preached a sermon so affecting "that nearly the whole assembly was melted to tears." However, within a month, Thomas Rawson Taylor was taken ill with tuberculosis and forced to resign his post as pastor. After a period of some recovery, he accepted a post as tutor at his alma mater, but again, illness forced him to resign.

Interestingly, he was traveling again at Christmas time from Sheffield to Nottingham when he was again invited to preach

at his old pulpit. He did so twice, and shortly after caught a severe cold that took his life.

The local newspaper wrote in great detail of his passing:

> "No minister ever loved his people more ardently or served them more faithfully than did he; and few ministers were more useful…. Whether seated in the cottages of the pious poor, or in the houses of the wealthy and learned, he was equally welcome, and entirely at home…. Age has often sat listening in silent admiration to his instructive discourse; and the spirit of the Christian has often been cheered in sorrow's darkest day by the heavenly consolations he administered and the tender sympathy he expressed."

Thomas Rawson Taylor was buried at Horton-Lane Chapel in Bradford, England, having passed at peace with his Maker. He was only 27 years old. In that short time, he had learned this great truth—God is love! It should also be mentioned that he was an accomplished poet who wrote out of the abundance of his heart. We sing one of his poems today.

Earth, with her ten thousand flow'rs,
Air, with all its beams and show'rs,
Heaven's infinite expanse,
Sea's resplendent countenance—
All around and all above
Bear this record: God is love.

Sounds among the vales and hills,
In the woods and by the rills,
Of the breeze and of the bird,
By the gentle murmur stirred—

Sacred songs, beneath, above,
Have one chorus: God is love.

All the hopes that sweetly start
From the fountain of the heart,
All the bliss that ever comes
To our earthly human homes,
All the voices from above
Sweetly whisper: God is love.

Sources:

https://www.newspapers.com/image/?clipping_id=2107916
1&fcfToken=eyJhbGciOiJIUzI1NiIsInR5cCI6IkpXVCJ9.
eyJmcmVlLXZpZXctaWQiOjQwMDg4MTQyMiwiaWF0I-
joxNjI5MjQxNzMzLCJleHAiOjE2MjkzMjgxMzN9.sXn-
JfMHASd7YWscHB8imtRM6JWzqdUAxTtqMfndMHlM

https://www.churchofjesuschrist.org/music/library/hymns/
god-is-love-women?lang=eng

THE CHRISTUS STATUE

CHAPTER THIRTY-FOUR

IN SEARCH OF CHRIST

There are many ways that followers of Jesus Christ search for means to express their love for him. Poetry, music, and art have been used as vehicles to express deep emotions and feelings for the Savior.

Albert Heinrich Hoffman was a language professor and librarian at the University of Breslau, Poland in the 1830's. He was part of a new generation of scholars who saw value in preserving and studying the art and literature of common people. Hoffman was traveling in Silesia, an area in central Europe. His purpose was to gather traditional songs of the region, some of which had religious themes. He heard a group of peasants singing a traditional folk song and he was impressed. Hoffman copied down both words and music from this oral recitation and published the song in his collection, *Schlesische Volkslieder*, in 1842. The union of the traditional folk tune and words praising the Savior made a beautiful song and a way for those people to celebrate their beliefs.

Very little was known of this song's origin, though some stories attributed it to being sung by 12th century German crusaders, a notion which historians believe is more legend than fact. Prior to Hoffman's publication, the text, author unknown, appeared in a German Roman Catholic hymnbook in 1677.

In another part of Europe, a Danish sculptor was searching for just the right way to portray Christ. Bertel Thorvaldsen was commissioned in 1819 to create a collection of statues of Christ and the twelve apostles for a renovation of the Lutheran Church of Our Lady, which had been damaged during the Napoleonic wars. Drawings and then clay models were originally used as he designed the sculpture of Christ.

According to J.M. Thiele, Thorvaldsen's biographer, the sculptor wrestled with the way he wanted to portray the Savior. The traditional pose of Christ's arms crossed upon His chest did not seem right. He expressed his frustration to one of his friends, who with a desire to help, outstretched his arms and asked what Thorvaldsen wanted to communicate with the design of the statue. As Thorvaldsen looked at his friend and contemplated an answer, he suddenly exclaimed, "I have it now! It shall be so!" Thus, according to Thiele, the conception of the statue was nothing short of divine inspiration. The arms of the Savior were designed to reach out and welcome whoever looked at Him.

The statue was originally made of clay and then plaster. A final version of the statue of Christ, along with sculptures of the twelve apostles, were made of Carrara marble from Italy, and placed in the Church of Our Lady in 1838. In Thorvaldsen's search to find the Savior, the statue became the crowning achievement of his life and is known throughout the world today as the Christus.

American Richard Storrs Willis, who graduated from Yale University, spent six years studying in Germany, searching for music which celebrated Christian beliefs. He encountered a well-known, simple, yet beautiful song about the Savior. Willis returned to the United States in 1848 and through his efforts, three verses of the song were translated into English and published in his book *Church Chorales and Choir Studies*

in 1850. Titled "Fairest Lord Jesus," the English words were matched with the traditional Silesian melody and a beautiful hymn was introduced to English speaking Christians.

Fairest Lord Jesus! Ruler of all nature!
O, Thou of God and man the Son!
Thee will I cherish, Thee will I honor,
Thou, my soul's glory, joy and crown!

Fair are the meadows, fairer still the woodlands,
Robed in the blooming garb of spring;
Jesus is fairer, Jesus is purer,
Who makes the woeful heart to sing.

Fair is the sunshine, fairer still the moonlight,
And all the twinkling starry host;
Jesus shines brighter, Jesus shines purer
Than all the angels heaven can boast.

Even Hungarian composer Franz Liszt was drawn to the hymn "Fairest Lord Jesus." He used the melody in a section of an oratorio he wrote in 1862.

The English version of the hymn still lacked a verse which had not been translated from the original German hymn. Lutheran pastor and theologian, Joseph A. Seiss, served congregations in Virginia, Maryland, and Pennsylvania. In searching for additional songs which honored the Savior, he found a fourth stanza to the German version of the hymn, which had previously been overlooked. The fourth verse was translated into English in 1873. Seiss renamed the song "Beautiful

Savior" in The Sunday School Book for the Use of Evangelical Lutheran Congregations.

The words of the final stanza of "Fairest Lord Jesus/Beautiful Savior" are a stirring benediction for Christians of all nations in search of Christ.

> *Beautiful Savior! Lord of all the nations!*
> *Son of God and Son of Man!*
> *Glory and honor, praise, adoration,*
> *Now and Forevermore be Thine.*

Sources:

https://hymnstudiesblog.wordpress.com/2008/05/16/quotfairest-lord-jesusquot/

http://drhamrick.blogspot.com/2013/11/fairest-lord-jesus.html

http://drhamrick.blogspot.com/2013/11/fairest-lord-jesus.html

https://www.umcdiscipleship.org/articles/history-of-hymns-fairest-lord-jesus

https://www.ldsliving.com/5-Things-You-Never-Knew-About-the-Christus-Statue/s/78222

https://www.thechurchnews.com/global/2019-01-14/from-copenhagen-to-rome-a-behind-the-scenes-look-at-the-italy-visitors-center-christus-statue-154992

CHARLES GABRIEL

CHAPTER THIRTY-FIVE

The Plowboy Composer

It is remarkable what the Lord can do with someone who has faith and is willing to use the talents they are given.

Charles Hutchinson Gabriel was born in 1856, one of seven children born to Iowa farmer parents—I. N. and Cleopatra Cotton Gabriel. In addition to farming near Sugar Creek, Iowa, Charles' father taught singing schools. Charles was about 10 years old before he saw his first musical instrument, which was a rough type of harpsichord.

From a young age, Charles showed a talent and love for music. At the age of 15, he made up his mind and announced to his mother that he wanted to be a songwriter. While working in the fields on the family farm, he would compose melodies in his mind and then write them down in the evening. One story suggested his musical talent was recognized in his boyhood hometown. The pastor of the church which his family attended saw Charles walking in town early in the week and asked him if he knew a good song to go along with the sermon topic for Sunday. By the end of the week, Charles had written a song for that Sunday with words and music.

When Charles was only sixteen, his father passed away, and the following year, he began to travel and lead his own singing schools. He later found employment teaching music in Texas and Oklahoma schools, worked at Grace Episcopal Methodist Church in San Francisco, and for a publishing firm in Chicago.

It is said that Charles loved to sing and wrote songs every day. Over the course of his life, it is believed that the prolific composer wrote over 8,000 songs, mostly hymns. During his life he edited 35 gospel song books, eight Sunday School song books, ten children's song books, and countless other music collections including anthems, cantatas, and instructional books. Not only was the man prolific in his compositions, but he demonstrated a powerful understanding of and love for the Lord and the scriptures.

Charles Hutchinson Gabriel earned a unique legacy in American hymn writing. His contemporaries called him the Prince of American Hymn Writers—and all of this from a man who never had a music lesson. This master of sacred music was taught his craft by the grace of God.

In 1898, he penned the words and wrote the music for this great Christian hymn.

> *I stand all amazed at the love Jesus offers me,*
> *Confused at the grace that so fully he proffers me.*
> *I tremble to know that for me he was crucified,*
> *That for me, a sinner, he suffered, he bled and died.*
>
> *Oh, it is wonderful that he should care for me,*
> *Enough to die for me!*
> *Oh, it is wonderful, wonderful to me!*

Charles Gabriel is a living legacy and testament to the very thing he wrote about—that the love and grace of the Savior will raise all of us, if we are willing, from humble obscurity, to exalted royalty.

Thank the Lord for the plowboy composer who became a prophet of music.

Sources:

https://archive.is/20130121190548/http://desmoinesregister.com/apps/pbcs.dll/article?AID=/99999999/FAMOUSIOWANS/501300335

https://www.thetabernaclechoir.org/articles/i-stand-all-amazed---video-and-lyrics.html

https://en.wikipedia.org/wiki/Charles_H._Gabriel

CHRIST WITH CHILDREN

CHAPTER THIRTY-SIX

A Sunday School Teacher for 35 Years

William Henry Parker was born the son of James and Hellen Parker in Basford, England in March 1845. His parents were working class people. Census records show that at the age of 16, William was a blacksmith apprentice and ten years later, a machine builder in a local lace factory. Notwithstanding his humble circumstances, William learned to read and write well. In time, he married Mary Ann and they had four children.

William became a member of the Chelsea Street Baptist Church in Basford, and in time was the superintendent and secretary of the Sunday School—a position he held for thirty-five years. William taught classes for the children and frequently wrote poems and hymns for the young. How does one volunteer and teach children the gospel for so many years and not love them?

It is said that one day in about 1885, William was teaching his class and the children asked him to tell them another story about Jesus. The request struck him and with inspiration William began to write:

> *Tell me the stories of Jesus I love to hear,*
> *Things I would ask him to tell me if he were here.*
> *Scenes by the wayside, tale of the sea,*
> *Stories of Jesus, tell them to me.*

First let me hear how the children stood 'round his knee,
And I shall fancy his blessings resting on me;
Words full of kindness, deeds full of grace,
All in the lovelight of Jesus' face.

Tell me, in accents of wonder, how rolled the sea,
Tossing a boat in a tempest on Galilee;
And how the Master, ready and kind,
Chided the billows and hushed the wind.

Into the city I'd follow the children's band,
Waving a branch of the palm tree high in my hand;
One of His heralds, Yes, I would sing
Loudest hosanna, "Jesus is King!"

From the kind teacher's pen flowed several simple, yet powerful verses, written from the perspective of a child's earnest seeking to know the Lord. The poem was titled "Tell Me the Stories of Jesus." In 1904, it was set to music.

William H. Parker died in the same place he was born—Basford, England, on December 2, 1929, and was buried there. It is said that he never travelled the world, but his humble hymn for children did. Around the world for more than 100 years, children and adults have been lifted closer to God by his hymn. You see, William comprehended a priceless principle that every teacher should know—that to know, love, and tell the stories of Jesus is to better know, love and serve Him.

Sources:

https://www.familysearch.org/tree/person/ordinances/GQK3-481

https://hymnary.org/text/tell_me_the_stories_of_jesus_i_love_to

https://www.hymns.com/store/pg/222-LME-2017-May-Hymn-of-the-Month.aspx

http://www.hymntime.com/tch/htm/t/m/t/s/tmtsoj.htm

https://www.thetabernaclechoir.org/articles/tell-me-the-stories-of-jesus-history.html

https://www.crosswalk.com/church/worship/tell-me-the-stories-of-jesus-11637764.html

http://www.hymntime.com/tch/bio/p/a/r/k/parker_wh.htm

CHARLES WESLEY

CHAPTER THIRTY-SEVEN

CHARLES AND HIS DAY OF PENTECOST

Saturday, May 20, 1738. A thirty-one-year-old minister of the Church of England named Charles was in terrible pain from pleurisy. But as agonizing as that pain was, the "agony" of his soul was worse. For many months he had labored, searched, and prayed to know the Savior—to find true faith and forgiveness. His soul hungered and thirsted after God. In his journal, some days previous, he wrote, "Sat., May 13th. I waked without Christ; yet still desirous of finding him."

Like so many others, young Charles knew of Christ, but did he truly know Him? "I longed to find Christ," he wrote "that I might show him to all mankind; that I might praise, that I might love him."

Hour after hour, day after day, Charles "labored, waited, and prayed to feel 'who loved me, and gave himself for [me.]'"And now on this day, a friend came and with feeling and emotion read Luke 9 and the story of the man with palsy borne of friends to the Master's side, who is then by the Savior's kindness healed. Upon hearing that tender story, Charles wrote, "I saw herein, and firmly believed, that his faith would be available for the healing of me."

The following day, Sunday, May 21, Charles rose and began to pray fervently, calling upon God for the promises contained in the scriptures, concluding, "Thou art God who canst not lie; I wholly rely upon thy most true promise: accomplish it in thy time and manner."

Charles then laid down and prepared himself to sleep. Just then, he heard the door to his room open and a woman's voice say, "In the name of Jesus of Nazareth, arise, and believe, and thou shalt be healed of all thy infirmities." The door closed and the woman, a Mrs. Musgrave, he deduced by the voice, slipped out. Charles said:

> "I wondered how it should enter into her head to speak in that manner. The words struck me to the heart. I sighed, and said within myself, 'O that Christ would but speak thus to me!' I lay musing and trembling: then thought, 'But what if it should be Him?'"

He sent for Mrs. Musgrave and asked if it was her. In response she said, "It was I, a weak, sinful creature, spoke; but the words were Christ's: he commanded me to say them, and so constrained me that I could not forbear."

Charles learned that she had experienced a singular dream at the same time he became so ill. In the dream, she heard a knock at the door, went down, and opened it. There she "saw a person in white." She asked him who he was and He replied, "I am Jesus Christ." The dream closed immediately and Mrs. Musgrave was at first frightened, but soon found herself, "full of the power of faith, so that she could scarce contain herself, and almost doubted whether she was sober. At the same time, she was enlarged in love and prayer for all mankind, and commanded to go and assure me from Christ of my recovery, soul and body."

She struggled with what she was prompted to do—did she, so weak and unworthy, dare share such promises with Charles, the minister? She told her brother of her dilemma and he replied sagely, "Go in the name of the Lord. Fear not! You're the

minister? Speak you the words: Christ will do the work. Out of the mouth of babes and sucklings hath he ordained strength."

She went, she spoke, and Charles believed and the promises were received. Charles was reborn from that moment forward. He would ever after refer to that as his "Day of Pentecost." Charles was consumed with a desire to share the gospel of Jesus Christ with the common man of the British Isles. He rose from his bed of affliction and with the remainder of his days, traveled and taught hundreds of thousands in open-air meetings.

It is not just for his traveling that he is remembered. For you see, not many days after his conversion, Charles composed a hymn. Though we do not know for sure what hymn that was, it was a beginning. Charles would go on to write more than 6,000 hymns of praise and the glory and doctrine of the Redeemer—more than any man before or since. Charles was Charles Wesley. Among those hymns, written about a year after his conversion, was this one—a hymn that shouts in joyous praise of the coming of Christ. Charles called it "A Hymn for Christmas Day," but you will recognize it differently.

Hark! The herald angels sing
Glory to the newborn King!
Peace on earth, and mercy mild,
God and sinners reconciled.
Joyful all ye nations rise,
Join the triumphs of the skies;
With the angelic host proclaim
Christ is born in Bethlehem.
Hark! The herald angels sing
Glory to the newborn King!

Hail the heaven-born Prince of Peace!
Hail the Son of Righteousness!
Light and life to all he brings,
Risen with healing in his wings.
Mild he lays his glory by,
Born that man no more may die;
Born to raise the sons of earth,
Born to give them second birth.
Hark! The herald angels sing
Glory to the newborn King!

Sources:

http://wesley.nnu.edu/charles-wesley/the-journal-of-charles-wesley-1707-1788/the-journal-of-charles-wesley-may-1-august-31-1738/

https://en.wikipedia.org/wiki/Hark!_The_Herald_Angels_Sing

https://en.wikipedia.org/wiki/Charles_Wesley

HENRY WADSWORTH LONGFELLOW

CHAPTER THIRTY-EIGHT

THERE IS NO PEACE

We live in the most troubled times of recent history. The hearts of men wax colder than they have ever been and darkness benights the minds and hearts of men the world over. The constant bombardment of media gloom steals our hope and destroys our peace, but it will not last! We have been here before.

1861 was a similarly dark, troubled, and uncertain time in the United States. Civil war loomed. Contention and hate divided the nation and threats abounded. Henry Wadsworth Longfellow, the acclaimed poet, wrote:

> "Six states have left the Union, led by South Carolina. President Buchanan is an antediluvian, an après-moi-le-déluge President, who does not care what happens, if he only gets safely through his term. We owe the present state of things mainly to him. He has sympathized with the disunionists. It is now too late to put the fire out. We must let it burn out."

Henry opposed slavery, but he opposed civil war even more. Then came word on April 12, 1861, "News comes that Fort Sumter is attacked. And the war begins! Who can foresee the end?" Peace was shattered by cannon fire and the world as they knew it was in sudden turmoil!

Then, on July 9, 1861, Henry's beloved wife, Fanny Appleton Longfellow was sealing some packages with hot wax when a match dropped to the floor and ignited her dress on fire. She ran to the study where Longfellow was and he attempted to put the fire out, but Fanny was badly burned and passed away the next day. Henry's grief was deep and prolonged, so much so that at times he feared that he would be sent to an asylum, so debilitating was it. One heavy year later, Henry wrote, "I can make no record of these days. Better leave them wrapped in silence. Perhaps someday God will give me peace."

If that were not enough, in March 1863, Henry's eldest son, Charles, age 19, boarded a train for Washington, D. C., and against his father's wishes, joined the Union Army. On December 1, 1863, Henry was sitting down to dinner at his Cambridge, Massachusetts home when he received a telegram that Charles had been severely wounded in the Battle of Mine Run. Henry quickly went south and brought his son home for what would be a lengthy recovery. Henry would summarize these days thus, "I have been through a great deal of trouble and anxiety."

It is out of this series of tragic events that on Christmas Day, 1864, Henry Wadsworth Longfellow penned the following words:

> *I heard the bells on Christmas Day*
> *Their old, familiar carols play,*
> *And wild and sweet*
> *The words repeat*
> *Of peace on earth, good will to men!*
>
> *I thought how, as the day had come,*
> *The belfries of all Christendom*

Had rolled along
The unbroken song
Of peace on earth, good will to men!

Till, ringing, singing on its way,
The world revolved from night to day,
A voice, a chime,
A chant sublime
Of peace on earth, good will to men!

The poem was written when the Civil War still tore at the nation's heart. When the poem was set to music in 1872, the next two stanzas of Longfellow's poem were left out as they have been in the singing of this sacred Christmas hymn ever since. However, they tell the full story behind the hymn. Longfellow continued:

Then from each black, accursed mouth
The cannon thundered in the South,
And with the sound
The carols drowned
Of peace on earth, good will to men!

It was as if an earthquake rent
The hearth-stones of a continent,
And made forlorn
The households born
Of peace on earth, good will to men!

And in despair I bowed my head;
"There is no peace on earth," I said:
"For hate is strong,

And mocks the song
Of peace on earth, good will to men!"

And it is here, like the pealing bells of Longfellow's church, that his message sounds with ringing clarity. He concluded:

Then pealed the bells more loud and deep:
"God is not dead; nor doth he sleep!
The wrong shall fail
The right prevail,
With peace on earth, good will to men!"

And so, it will be for us! God is not dead! The wrong and all who support it, will fail, and the righteousness of Jesus Christ will prevail with peace. Have no fear!

Sources:

https://www.hymnologyarchive.com/i-heard-the-bells-on-christmas-day

https://www.battlefields.org/learn/articles/christmas-bells

https://www.mentalfloss.com/article/72869/how-civil-war-inspired-i-heard-bells-christmas-day

https://en.wikipedia.org/wiki/Henry_Wadsworth_Longfellow

https://www.thegospelcoalition.org/blogs/justin-taylor/the-story-of-pain-and-hope-behind-i-heard-the-bells-on-christmas-day/

SPANISH-AMERICAN WAR SOLDIERS

CHAPTER THIRTY-NINE

CHRISTMAS MORNING

The lyrics and melody of a hymn have the power to unite and comfort believers—even in the most unlikely places. This was the case with a hymn first published in England in 1787.

On Christmas Eve in 1898, a memorable moment in time touched the lives of United States soldiers who were serving in the Spanish-American War. Northerners and Southerners, blacks and whites, served together on the island of Cuba, more than thirty years after the United States Civil War. Lieutenant Colonel Curtis Guild, Jr. was serving as Inspector General of the Seventh Army Corps near Havana and described this incident.

It was a balmy, tropical night, and he, like many of his comrades, were talking of Christmas and home. Memories of family, sweethearts, and the celebrations of the season were surely part of their conversations. As the clock struck twelve to welcome Christmas Day, from the camp of the Forty-Ninth Iowa came a sentinel's call, "Number ten; twelve o'clock and all's well!"

The sentinel's call had barely finished, when from the bandsmen's tents of the same regiment there arose the music of an old, familiar hymn. This hymn, which first made its way to America from England in 1820, was frequently sung in many Christian churches. Northern soldiers would have learned this song as children from their mothers. To Southern

soldiers, it was not only a beloved song, but the favorite hymn of General Robert E. Lee, and was sung at his funeral.

A single baritone voice started the song. Another voice joined in, and soon the whole regiment was singing—the Sixth Missouri followed, then the Fourth Virginia, and soon all of the rest of the army spanning the ridges of the camp. However, the song was not one of the popular Christmas carols of the day, but the words written more than 100 years earlier by a believer only identified as "K---", who trusted in God and His promises. All of the verses would have been familiar to most of these men, but this verse particularly was mentioned by Lieutenant Colonel Guild.

> *Fear not, I am with thee, O be not dismayed;*
> *For I am thy God, and will still give thee aide;*
> *I'll strengthen thee, help thee, and cause thee to stand,*
> *Upheld by My righteous, omnipotent hand.*

The hymn, "How Firm a Foundation," brought comfort and unity to American soldiers that Christmas morning. It has been published in over 1,900 hymnals and provided consolation and hope to Christians for over 200 years. The final verse states:

> *The soul that on Jesus hath leaned for repose*
> *I will not, I cannot, desert to his foes;*
> *That soul, though all hell should endeavor to shake,*
> *I'll never, no never, no never forsake!*

Sources:

https://hymnary.org/text/how_firm_a_foundation_ye_saints_of

https://reasonabletheology.org/hymn-story-how-firm-a-foundation/

Benson, L. F. 1903. Studies of Familiar Hymns. Philadelphia, The Westminster Press.

OBENDORF, AUSTRIA

CHAPTER FORTY

The Priest of the Poor

Joseph Franz Mohr was born in Salzburg, Austria on 11 December 1792. Joseph grew up without his father—just his mother, grandmother, and a stepsister. Notwithstanding their poverty, Joseph displayed uncommon talent and intelligence and was sponsored to obtain a university education, where at the same time, he sang in the choir and played the violin.

After graduation in 1811, he enrolled in the seminary to become a priest, which required special permission from the church. Permission was granted and by 1815, he was ordained a priest at the age of 23. In that same year, he was appointed assistant priest in Mariapfurr. It was there, in 1816, that he wrote these now famous words:

Silent Night, Holy Night!
All is calm, all is bright,
Round yon virgin mother and child.
Holy infant so tender and mild.
Sleep in heavenly peace;
Sleep in heavenly peace.

Silent night! Holy night!
Shepherds quake at the sight!
Glories stream from heaven afar;

Heave'nly hosts sing Alleluia!
Christ, the Savior, is born!
Christ, the Savior, is born!

Silent night! Holy night!
Son of God, love's pure light
Radiant beams from thy holy face,
With the dawn of redeeming grace,
Jesus, Lord, at thy birth;
Jesus, Lord, at thy birth.

On August 25, 1817, Joseph Mohr became the assistant priest in the new parish of Oberndorf. It was there that he met and became friends with Franz Xaver Gruber, who oversaw the choir and organ at the St. Nikola Church.

Just before Christmas 1818, Joseph Mohr brought the poem he had written to Franz Gruber and asked him to compose a melody. Gruber agreed and wrote a most fitting and tender melody, and together the two friends sang the song for the first time in the church at St. Nikola following the Christmas Mass. Joseph accompanied on the guitar.

From there, Joseph Mohr went on to a life of dedicated service to the church and his people. He became known as the "Priest of the Poor." He passed away December 4, 1848. "His only estate was his guitar." Joseph Mohr "never witnessed the success that his Christmas hymn would have throughout the world."

And just one more thing…the Christmas hymn, "Silent Night" is Christmas! It captures our hearts and souls and invokes the peace that was the wondrous birth of the Prince of Peace. Maybe it is altogether fitting that Joseph Mohr was

given those meaningful words, for you see, Joseph Mohr's birth was considered a "crime." He was born out of wedlock, abandoned by his father, shunned by society, and stigmatized by his church. And yet, like the Master he served, he loved and lifted the children of the poor.

Sources:

https://www.stillenacht.com/en/protagonists/joseph-mohr-1792-1848/

https://www.german-way.com/history-and-culture/holidays-and-celebrations/christmas/stille-nacht-silent-night/

JEREMIAH RANKIN

CHAPTER FORTY-ONE

TILL WE MEET AGAIN

Inspiration to write the words of a song can come in many ways. For one text, the simple meaning of a frequently used word in the English language became the catalyst for a beloved hymn.

Jeremiah Rankin was a pastor at the First Congregational Church and president of Howard University in Washington, D.C. In 1882, he was looking for a song which he could use at the end of his Sunday evening choir meetings—something that would be a good benediction to sing as the members left for the night. None of the hymns seemed quite right, so Dr. Rankin decided to write his own song. He looked up the origin of the term good-bye and saw that its meaning was "God be with you." With that thought in mind, he wrote eight verses of a hymn which he titled "God Be with You Till We Meet Again." He sent the lyrics to William Tomer, a public school music teacher in New Jersey and music director at Grace Methodist Episcopal Church, who composed just the right melody. Jeremiah Rankin said, "It was written as a Christian good-bye." This closing song for his choir to sing as they parted has been published in over 1,000 hymnals today.

It is fitting that this song has become one of the signature pieces of a group President Ronald Reagan referred to as "America's Choir." The world-famous Tabernacle Choir at Temple Square was founded in 1847. Composer John Williams said of the choir, "These are people who are there

for the joy of music. It's not a job with them; it's a mission." The choir began weekly Sunday morning broadcasts of *Music and the Spoken Word* in 1929. The tradition of closing each choir broadcast with "God Be with You Till We Meet Again" is a long one. However, the retirement of the choir's eleventh conductor, Richard P. Condie, unwittingly started a new tradition of the music conductor singing, rather than leading, this song. On his last broadcast before retiring, wanting to avoid fanfare or attention, Condie simply gave the choir the downbeat of the song, put down his baton, and walked out of the Tabernacle. Since that day, the conductor has put down his baton and faced the audience, joining with the choir in singing, "God Be with You Till We Meet Again."

> *God be with you till we meet again;*
> *By his counsels guide, uphold you;*
> *With his sheep securely fold you.*
> *God be with you till we meet again.*
>
> *Till we meet, till we meet*
> *Till we meet at Jesus' feet,*
> *Till we meet, till we meet,*
> *God be with you till we meet again.*

This hymn often has a personal connection to many Christians as they bid farewell to those who mean so much to them. Musician and composer Jason Tonioli wrote:

> "This song has a direct connection to my tear ducts. After serving for several months in a city in Argentina as a missionary, I was at the bus station ready to leave. A large group of friends and fellow church members

had gathered to tell me good-bye and emotions were high. As it came time to load the bus, these wonderful people began singing "God Be with You Till We Meet Again." My eyes filled with tears as I slowly climbed the stairs of the bus and looked back at my friends for one last time.

The most personal time for me to play this song was at my own father's funeral. I am grateful for the knowledge that we will meet again and be with the Savior."

The song which Jeremiah Rankin wrote as a simple good-bye, to be sung on parting by friends, has exceeded any expectation which he ever had. He was very pleased when it became the official closing song of the Young People's Society of Christian Endeavor. Were he here today and could see the impact of his song over more than a century, I think he would echo to us what he said to the young people, "Long, long may they sing it."

Sources:

https://hymnary.org/text/god_be_with_you_till_we_meet_again

https://www.thetabernaclechoir.org/articles/former-choir-conductor-walked-out-of-tabernacle.html?cid=facebook-shared

https://www.thetabernaclechoir.org/articles/god-be-with-you-till-we-meet-again.html

http://plymouthbrethren.org/article/10394

Index of Hymns

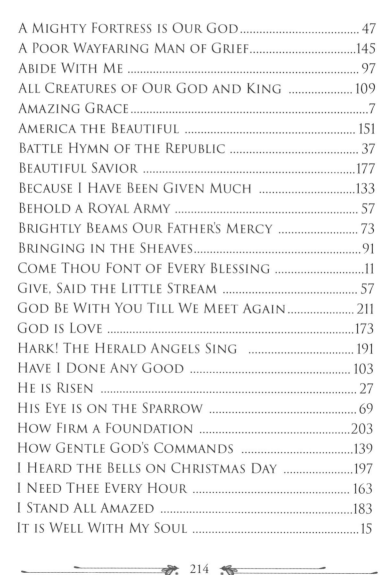

About The
Authors

Glenn Rawson has been telling stories for over 30 years. He started writing as a way to share his thoughts with family and a few close friends. An acquaintance who worked in radio asked him to record and share his stories with his audience. Listeners enjoyed hearing them, and the recordings quickly spread to dozens of other stations throughout the country.

Glenn has authored more than 20 books and written and produced over 100 TV documentaries. Over the years, he has connected with millions of people through print, radio and TV broadcasts, and online social media channels.

Glenn loves to research and write, but is happiest when he is traveling the world as a tour guide, sharing stories of history and the communities he visits with his guests. His goal is to help inspire and lift others with his stories.

Glenn and his wife Debbie have seven children and eighteen grandchildren.

For information about receiving weekly stories and other books available, please visit glennrawsonstories.com or historyofthesaints.org.

JEAN TONIOLI

Jean worked as an educator for more than 30 years, and even in retirement works as adjunct faculty at Weber State University to mentor student teachers. She has always had an affinity for finding, researching, and sharing stories about her ancestors, helping to ensure their memory carries on with her family. She has four children and eight grandchildren.

Jean has a special love for piano and choir music. Her children can all recount stories of how their mother would sit at the piano bench to ensure each child would learn to play the piano. Her encouragement paid off when her son Jason started writing and arranging music.

Her talents for researching, to find stories about many of the composers featured in this book, writing, and editing have been invaluable.

JASON TONIOLI

Jason is best known for his piano hymn arrangements. His career started in banking and marketing, and then he founded a successful software and consulting company. Throughout that time, he wrote several piano books and recorded and released multiple piano albums.

After the sale of his company in 2018, he was able to spend more time on his music and as of 2021 has released 14 piano solo books and 12 recorded albums. His music has been played well over 100 million times.

He lives in Utah with his wife and four children and spends as much time being a dad as possible.